Authors:
William K. Cross
Resource Specialist
Science/Math/Technology

J.R.Cross
Educational Consultant

Illustrator:
Keith Vasconcelles

Editors:
Evan D. Forbes, M.S. Ed.
Walter Kelly, M.A.

Senior Editor:
Sharon Coan, M.S. Ed.

Art Direction:
Elayne Roberts

Product Manager:
Phil Garcia

Imaging:
Holly Terrell

Photo Cover Credit:
Images provided by
PhotoDisc ©1994

Research:
Bobbie Johnson

Publishers:
Rachelle Cracchiolo, M.S. Ed.
Mary Dupuy Smith, M.S. Ed.

Hands-On Minds-On Science

Endangered Species

Primary

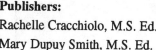

Teacher Created Materials, Inc.
P.O. Box 1040
Huntington Beach, CA 92647
©1994 Teacher Created Materials, Inc.
Made in U.S.A.

ISBN-1-55734-628-3

Table of Contents

Introduction..4

The Scientific Method...5

Science-Process Skills..7

Organizing Your Unit...9

What Does It Mean To Be Threatened, Endangered, or Extinct?

Just the Facts 11

Hands-On Activities
- A Species with Class...12
- Yummy Mathematics 14
- Diamasaurs...16
- Piecing Together Endangered Species 18
- Coding all Species..21

How Does a Species Become Threatened, Endangered, or Extinct?

Just the Facts..23

Hands-On Activities
- Yucky Water..24
- Guess Where I Live 26
- Tips on Trees...28
- Adding It all Up..30
- A Dwindling Classroom Habitat..32
- Beak Coordination 34
- How Big Is Big?..36
- Fishy Manipulative...37

Why Protect Threatened and Endangered Species?

Just the Facts..39

Hands-On Activities
- Food Chain Mobile 40
- Nature's Missing Links 46
- Power of Nature 48
- Pollution Diffusion Disaster...50
- Recycling—Mathematically Profitable..52
- At Home Conservation..55
- Door Knob Hanging Tree 57

Table of Contents *(cont.)*

How Can We Help Our Plant and Animal Friends?

Just the Facts 59
Hands-On Activities
- Lefty and Righty—Not All Right 60
- Window Terrarium Greenhouse 62
- Products: Short-Lived or Long-Lived 64
- Classroom Recycling Bins 66

Station-to-Station Activities

- Observe 68
- Communicate 70
- Compare 71
- Order 72
- Categorize 73
- Relate 74
- Infer 75
- Apply 76

Management Tools

- Science Safety 78
- Endangered Species Journal 79
- Endangered Species Observation Area 85
- Assessment Forms 86
- Science Award 89
- Organizations and Agencies 90

Threatened, Endangered, and Extinct Species 92

Glossary 93

Bibliography 95

What Is Science?

What Is Science?

What is science to young children? Is it something that they know is a part of their world? Is it a textbook in the classroom? Is it a tadpole changing into a frog? Is it a sprouting seed, a rainy day, a boiling pot, a turning wheel, a pretty rock, or a moonlit sky? Is science fun and filled with wonder and meaning? What does science mean to young children?

Science offers you and your eager children opportunities to explore the world around you and to make connections between the things you experience. The world becomes your classroom, and you, the teacher, a guide.

Science can, and should, fill children with wonder. It should cause them to be filled with questions and the desire to discover the answers to their questions. And, once they have discovered the answers, they should be actively seeking new questions to answer!

The books in this series give you and your children the opportunity to learn from the whole of your experience—the sights, sounds, smells, tastes, and touches, as well as what you read, write about, and do. This whole science approach allows you to experience and understand your world as you explore science concepts and skills together.

What Is An Endangered Species?

Endangered species are plants and animals whose numbers are becoming so low that the probability of their fading from existence is dangerously high. There are many causes for species extinction— wildlife trade, deforestation, exploding human populations, and increases in food production, to name just a few. It is often easy to take plants and animals for granted. They are everywhere—in our homes, our schools, our yards, our parks, our beaches. Life on earth depends on plants and animals in more ways than we can think of. It is impossible to come up with a well defined estimate of species extinction because the original number of species is unknown. However, we do know that species extinction is proceeding considerably faster than it did prior to 1800.

Through the activities in this book, children will learn about the concerns of the long-term health of the world's species. They will not only learn facts, but they will also learn how to apply those facts.

Most importantly, this unit will help us realize that we have inherited a world of boundless wonder and beauty. Children can learn that with knowledge and respect of their beautiful world, it is possible to live side by side with nature so that all species on earth can have a chance to survive.

The Scientific Method

The "scientific method" is one of several creative and systematic processes for proving or disproving a given question, following an observation. When the "scientific method" is used in the classroom, a basic set of guiding principles and procedures is followed in order to answer a question. However, real world science is often not as rigid as the "scientific method" would have us believe.

This systematic method of problem solving will be described in the paragraphs that follow.

1 Make an OBSERVATION.

The teacher presents a situation, gives a demonstration, or reads background material that interests students and prompts them to ask questions. Or students can make observations and generate questions on their own as they study a topic.

Example: Show students a movie about endangered species.

2 Select a QUESTION to investigate.

In order for students to select a question for a scientific investigation, they will have to consider the materials they have or can get, as well as the resources (books, magazines, people, etc.) actually available to them. You can help them make an inventory of their materials and resources, either individually or as a group.

Tell students that in order to successfully investigate the questions they have selected, they must be very clear about what they are asking. Discuss effective questions with your students. Depending upon their level, simplify the question or make it more specific.

Example: What does it mean when a species becomes threatened, endangered, or extinct?

3 Make a PREDICTION (Hypothesis).

Explain to students that a hypothesis is a good guess about what the answer to a question will probably be. But they do not want to make just any arbitrary guess. Encourage students to predict what they think will happen and why.

In order to formulate a hypothesis, students may have to gather more information through research.

Have students practice making hypotheses with questions you give them. Tell them to pretend they have already done their research. You want them to write each hypothesis so it follows these rules:

1. It is to the point.
2. It tells what will happen, based on what the question asks.
3. It follows the subject/verb relationship of the question.

Example: I think when a species becomes endangered, there are not many of them left.

The Scientific Method *(cont.)*

4 | Develop a **PROCEDURE** to test the hypothesis.

The first thing students must do in developing a procedure (the test plan) is to determine the materials they will need.

They must state exactly what needs to be done in step-by-step order. If they do not place their directions in the right order, or if they leave out a step, it becomes difficult for someone else to follow their directions. A scientist never knows when other scientists will want to try the same experiment to see if they end up with the same results!

Example: By simulating this activity, students will watch the numbers of species (classmates) disappear before their eyes.

5 | Record the **RESULTS** of the investigation in written and picture form.

The results (data collected) of a scientific investigation are usually expressed two ways—in written form and in picture form. Both are summary statements. The written form reports the results with words. The picture form (often a chart or graph) reports the results so the information can be understood at a glance.

Example: The results of this investigation can be recorded on a data-capture sheet provided (page 13).

6 | State a **CONCLUSION** that tells what the results of the investigation mean.

The conclusion is a statement which tells the outcome of the investigation. It is drawn after the student has studied the results of the experiment, and it interprets the results in relation to the stated hypothesis. A conclusion statement may read something like either of the following: "The results show that the hypothesis is supported," or "The results show that the hypothesis is not supported." Then restate the hypothesis if it was supported or revise it if it was not supported.

Example: The hypothesis that stated "when a species becomes endangered, there are not many of them left" is supported (or not supported).

7 | Record **QUESTIONS, OBSERVATIONS,** and **SUGGESTIONS** for future investigations.

Students should be encouraged to reflect on the investigations that they complete. These reflections, like those of professional scientists, may produce questions that will lead to further investigations.

Example: Can a species ever turn around from being endangered to not being endangered?

Science-Process Skills

Even the youngest students blossom in their ability to make sense out of their world and succeed in scientific investigations when they learn and use the science-process skills. These are the tools that help children think and act like professional scientists.

The first five process skills on the list below are the ones that should be emphasized with young children, but all of the skills will be utilized by anyone who is involved in scientific study.

Observing

It is through the process of observation that all information is acquired. That makes this skill the most fundamental of all the process skills. Children have been making observations all their lives, but they need to be made aware of how they can use their senses and prior knowledge to gain as much information as possible from each experience. Teachers can develop this skill in children by asking questions and making statements that encourage precise observations.

Communicating

Humans have developed the ability to use language and symbols which allow them to communicate not only in the "here and now" but also over time and space as well. The accumulation of knowledge in science, as in other fields, is due to this process skill. Even young children should be able to understand the importance of researching others' communications about science and the importance of communicating their own findings in ways that are understandable and useful to others. The endangered species journal and the data-capture sheets used in this book are two ways to develop this skill.

Comparing

Once observation skills are heightened, students should begin to notice the relationships between things that they are observing. *Comparing* means noticing similarities and differences. By asking how things are alike and different or which is smaller or larger, teachers will encourage children to develop their comparison skills.

Ordering

Other relationships that students should be encouraged to observe are the linear patterns of seriation (order along a continuum: e.g., rough to smooth, large to small, bright to dim, few to many) and sequence (order along a time line or cycle). By ranking graphs, time lines, cyclical and sequence drawings, and by putting many objects in order by a variety of properties, students will grow in their abilities to make precise observations about the order of nature.

Categorizing

When students group or classify objects or events according to logical rationale, they are using the process skill of categorizing. Students begin to use this skill when they group by a single property such as color. As they develop this skill, they will be attending to multiple properties in order to make categorizations; the animal classification system, for example, is one system students can categorize.

Science-Process Skills *(cont.)*

Relating

Relating, which is one of the higher-level process skills, requires student scientists to notice how objects and phenomena interact with one another and the change caused by these interactions. An obvious example of this is the study of chemical reactions.

Inferring

Not all phenomena are directly observable, because they are out of humankind's reach in terms of time, scale, and space. Some scientific knowledge must be logically inferred based on the data that is available. Much of the work of paleontologists, astronomers, and those studying the structure of matter is done by inference.

Applying

Even very young, budding scientists should begin to understand that people have used scientific knowledge in practical ways to change and improve the way we live. It is at this application level that science becomes meaningful for many students.

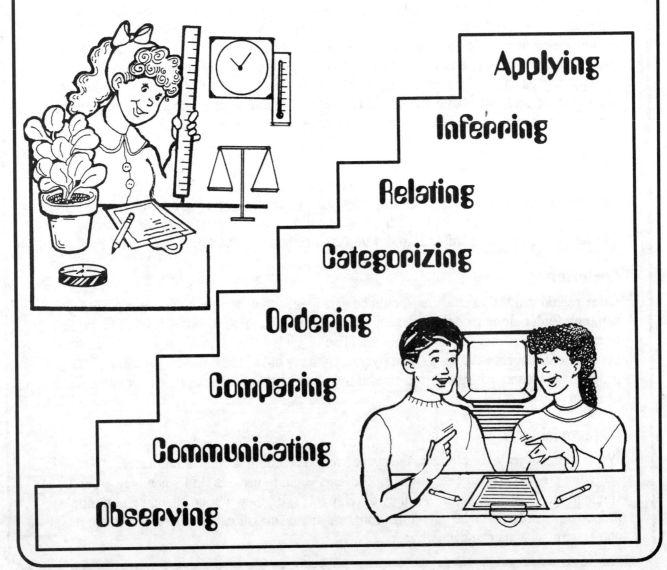

Applying

Inferring

Relating

Categorizing

Ordering

Comparing

Communicating

Observing

Organizing Your Unit

Designing a Science Lesson

In addition to the lessons presented in this unit, you will want to add lessons of your own, lessons that reflect the unique environment in which you live, as well as the interests of your students. When designing new lessons or revising old ones, try to include the following elements in your planning:

Question

Pose a question to your students that will guide them in the direction of the experiment you wish to perform. Encourage all answers, but you want to lead the students towards the experiment you are going to be doing. Remember, there must be an observation before there can be a question. (Refer to The Scientific Method, pages 5-6.)

Setting the Stage

Prepare your students for the lesson. Brainstorm to find out what students already know. Have children review books to discover what is already known about the subject. Invite them to share what they have learned.

Materials Needed for Each Group or Individual

List the materials each group or individual will need for the investigation. Include a data-capture sheet when appropriate.

Procedure

Make sure students know the steps to take to complete the activity. Whenever possible, ask them to determine the procedure. Make use of assigned roles in group work. Create (or have your students create) a data-capture sheet. Ask yourself, "How will my students record and report what they have discovered? Will they tally, measure, draw, or make a checklist? Will they make a graph? Will they need to preserve specimens?" Let students record results orally, using a video or audio tape recorder. For written recording, encourage students to use a variety of paper supplies such as poster board or index cards. It is also important for students to keep a journal of their investigation activities. Journals can be made of lined and unlined paper. Students can design their own covers. The pages can be stapled or be put together with brads or spiral binding.

Extensions

Continue the success of the lesson. Consider which related skills or information you can tie into the lesson, like math, language arts skills, or something being learned in social studies. Make curriculum connections frequently and involve the students in making these connections. Extend the activity, whenever possible, to home investigations.

Closure

Encourage students to think about what they have learned and how the information connects to their own lives. Prepare endangered species journals using directions on page 79. Provide an ample supply of blank and lined pages for students to use as they complete the Closure activities. Allow time for students to record their thoughts and pictures in their journals.

Organizing Your Unit *(cont.)*

Structuring Student Groups for Scientific Investigations

Using cooperative learning strategies in conjunction with hands-on and discovery learning methods will benefit all the students taking part in the investigation.

Cooperative Learning Strategies

1. In cooperative learning, all group members need to work together to accomplish the task.
2. Cooperative learning groups should be heterogeneous.
3. Cooperative learning activities need to be designed so that each student contributes to the group and individual group members can be assessed on their performance.
4. Cooperative learning teams need to know the social as well as the academic objectives of a lesson.

Cooperative Learning Groups

Groups can be determined many ways for the scientific investigations in your class. Here is one way of forming groups that has proven to be successful in primary classrooms.

- **The Team Leader**—scientist in charge of reading directions and setting up equipment.
- **The Biologist**—scientist in charge of carrying out directions (can be more than one student).
- **The Stenographer**—scientist in charge of recording all of the information.
- **The Transcriber**—scientist who translates notes and communicates findings.

If the groups remain the same for more than one investigation, require each group to vary the people chosen for each job. All group members should get a chance to try each job at least once.

Using Centers for Scientific Investigations

Set up stations for each investigation. To accommodate several groups at a time, stations may be duplicated for the same investigation. Each station should contain directions for the activity, all necessary materials (or a list of materials for investigators to gather), a list of words (a word bank) which students may need for writing and speaking about the experience, and any data-capture sheets or needed materials for recording and reporting data and findings.

Station-to-Station Activities are on pages 68-77. Model and demonstrate each of the activities for the whole group. Have directions at each station. During the modeling session, have a student read the directions aloud while the teacher carries out the activity. When all students understand what they must do, let small groups conduct the investigations at the centers. You may wish to have a few groups working at the centers while others are occupied with other activities. In this case, you will want to set up a rotation schedule so all groups have a chance to work at the centers.

Assign each team to a station, and after they complete the task described, help them rotate in a clockwise order to the other stations. If some groups finish earlier than others, be prepared with another unit-related activity to keep students focused on main concepts. After all rotations have been made by all groups, come together as a class to discuss what was learned.

Just the Facts

EXTINCT: Any living thing that disappears entirely and can no longer be found anywhere on earth is known as extinct—gone forever—like the dinosaurs, carrier pigeon, and the dodo bird. These organisms failed to adapt to a changing world or fell victim to oncoming circumstances, such as natural catastrophes or human intervention.

ENDANGERED SPECIES: When a species is put in the category of being endangered, it means that species may soon be unable to continue. Examples of some endangered species are the African elephant and black rhinoceros.

ENDANGERED SPECIES LIST: Today many people—scientists, conservationists, wildlife groups and organizations, along with governments—work hard to help prevent extinction of our wildlife. When they notice that a particular animal or plant is getting into trouble, it is placed on the endangered species list so people can start working to solve the problems that place such plants and animals in danger of extinction.

THREATENED SPECIES: A threatened species will most likely become an endangered species unless the circumstances surrounding that species change. For example, the Monarch butterfly was once a threatened species because their migration habitat was being destroyed for lumber. The government and lumber companies banded together and solved the problem.

Today, everyone should be working to get species off the endangered list and into another category called *delisted.* "Enlist to Delist." Once the white pelican was listed as endangered because its food was poisoned by DDT and its nesting grounds disturbed by people. There were few left. But action was taken, and laws were passed to ban DDT and protect their nesting sites. Today the white pelican is delisted.

Threatened

Endangered

Extinct

A Species with Class

Question

What does it mean when a species becomes *threatened, endangered,* or *extinct?*

Setting the Stage

- Tell students that unless current trends change, one can easily predict that many threatened species will soon be considered endangered and could more than likely become extinct.
- Have your class brainstorm a fictitious species name to represent themselves. It could resemble an animal, plant, or combination.

Materials Needed for Each Individual

- red, yellow, brown, and black squares of construction paper (nine equal sized squares of each color)
- scissors
- colored markers or crayons
- data-capture sheet (page 13)

Procedure

1. Have students help pass out the squares of red, yellow, brown, and black construction paper. With an average class size of 36, this would be one square per student. If class size is 32, then use eight squares of each color.
2. Have all students with red or yellow squares come to the front of the room. The 18 remaining students now represent what their class species would be like if it were *threatened.*
3. Now, have all students with brown squares come to the front of the room. The remaining nine seated students now represent their class species as if they were *endangered.*
4. Have the remaining nine students holding black squares come to the front of the room. The entire class will now look at 36 empty desks. Not one of the class species remains. This class species is gone forever and is now *extinct.*
5. Have students graph the fraction value of each stage of this activity on their data-capture sheets. The entire class is represented by the whole pie. A complete whole pie graph represents the class species. Next, have them color half the graph to represent threatened species, three-quarters of the graph to represent an endangered class species, and all the graph to represent the extinction of the class species.

Extensions

- Have students orally distinguish the meaning of *threatened, endangered,* and *extinct.*
- Have students reenact this activity at home for their families.

Closure

In their endangered species journals, have students write what it means to be *threatened, endangered,* and *extinct.*

A Species with Class *(cont.)*

Complete the pie graphs with the information from your experience.

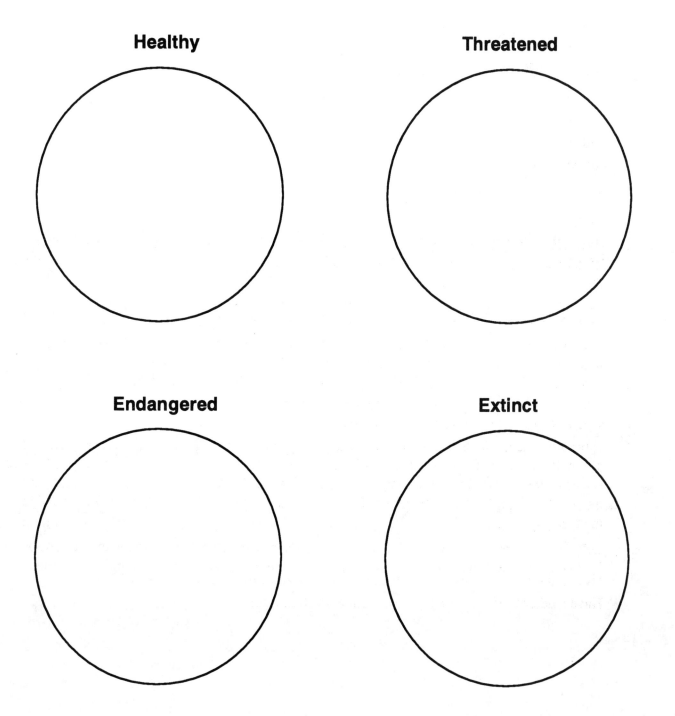

Healthy

Threatened

Endangered

Extinct

Yummy Mathematics

Question

What is the difference between natural extinction and accelerated extinction?

Setting the Stage

Tell students that in the distant past it took millions of years before a species became endangered and finally extinct. In most cases whole new species took over or evolved to fill the places of the old ones. In today's world, extinction is happening at a much more rapid rate, and new species cannot fill the vacancies because they have not had enough time to evolve or change over time.

Materials Needed for Each Group

- small bag of M & M's®
- stopwatch
- data-capture sheet (page 15)

Procedure

1. Have students eat one M & M® at a time, counting how many swallows to finish their bag. Then have students record this information on their data-capture sheets.

2. Have students also time how long it took to finish their bag and record this information on their data-capture sheets.

3. You will now eat a bag of M & M's® starting with one, then 2, 4, 6, and 8 until the bag is finished.

4. Have students count the swallows and time how long it takes for you to finish one bag. Then have them record this information on their data-capture sheets.

5. Have students compare the times and numbers of swallows between the students and you. Have them imagine their bag of M & M's® represents *natural* extinction and their teacher's bag represents *accelerated* extinction.

Extension

Have students research two species that became extinct by natural means and two species that became extinct due to acceleration.

Closure

By becoming aware and caring for our plants and animals we can play an important part in reducing the number of species that are on the brink of extinction. In their endangered species journals, have students write what they think might be some causes of accelerated extinction.

Yummy Mathematics *(cont.)*

Fill in the chart with the information needed.

	How Many Swallows?	How Long?
Students		
Teacher		

Tell how the numbers above can represent a *natural* rate of extinction and an *accelerated* rate of extinction.

_____

_____

_____

_____

Diamasaurs

Question
Would you like to be a scientist who studies and puts together skeletons or fossils of dinosaurs?

Setting the Stage
- Discuss with students that scientists who study and reconstruct skeletons or fossils of dinosaurs are called paleontologists. These scientists have put together dinosaurs ranging in size from 3'-100' (1m-33m) long.
- Have students define the term *paleontologist.*

Materials Needed for Each Student
- puzzle of "diamasaur" (page 17)
- scissors
- construction paper
- glue stick

Procedure
1. Distribute "diamasaur" puzzles, scissors, glue, and construction paper to each student.
2. Have students cut out all the diamond pieces and reconstruct the two dinosaurs on a backing of construction paper.
3. Have them glue the pieces down when correctly placed.

Extensions
- Have students research and identify the name of the dinosaur in their puzzles.
- Have students display their completed "diamasaurs" on the walls of your classroom.
- Provide your students with a pattern so that they can create their own "diamasaurs."

Closure
In their endangered species journals, have students investigate two other dinosaurs. Information that should be included is their names, sizes, what they eat, and their enemies.

Diamasaurs *(cont.)*

Cut out your "diamasaur" puzzle pieces.

Piecing Together Endangered Species

Question

Can you piece together the endangered species pictured on the following page, using the seven tangram pieces on the pattern found on page 20?

Setting the Stage

- Discuss with students some specifics pertaining to the endangerment of hawks, crocodiles, and turtles. Include where these animals live, what they eat, who they are prey to, and why they are endangered.

- Tell students that tangrams are the seven pieces derived from a perfect square pattern. The square pattern is easily manipulated mathematically and is often used to determine areas, perimeters, and geometric forms of common shapes. The square is comprised of five triangles—two small equal-sized triangles, one medium-sized triangle, and two large equal-sized triangles. The two remaining pieces are parallelograms—one being a perfect small square or diamond and the other being a small rhombohedron. (See pattern illustration on page 20.)

Materials Needed for Each Individual

- tangram pattern sheet (page 19)
- construction paper
- tangram (page 20)
- glue stick
- scissors

Note to the teacher: Art is often integrated with math and science by using the tangram pieces to represent thematic illustrations. In this case, students will design illustrations of endangered species such as crocodiles, hawks, and turtles.

Procedure

1. Have students cut out the shapes making up the square tangram on page 20.
2. Have them design the illustrations of the endangered species you have provided them (page 19).
3. Once they have designed an acceptable depiction, have them mount their pictures on construction paper using a glue stick.
4. Have them label and describe the endangered species they have designed.

Extensions

- Allow students the opportunity to design their own samples of endangered species, using the tangram shapes.
- Have students report on one of the three endangered species from their tangram pattern page.

Closure

In their endangered species journals, have students write a dialogue between two of the above endangered species. Let the animals express their thoughts about improving their situation.

Piecing Together Endangered Species *(cont.)*

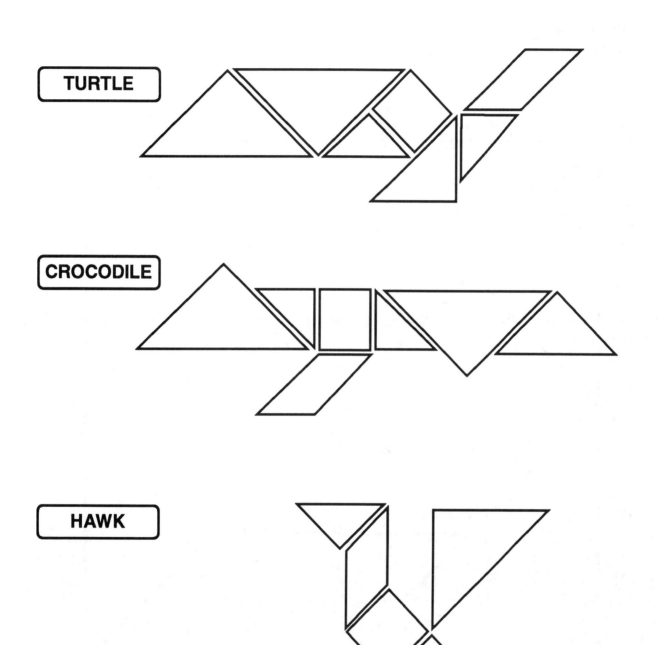

TURTLE

CROCODILE

HAWK

Piecing Together Endangered Species *(cont.)*

Cut out your tangram.

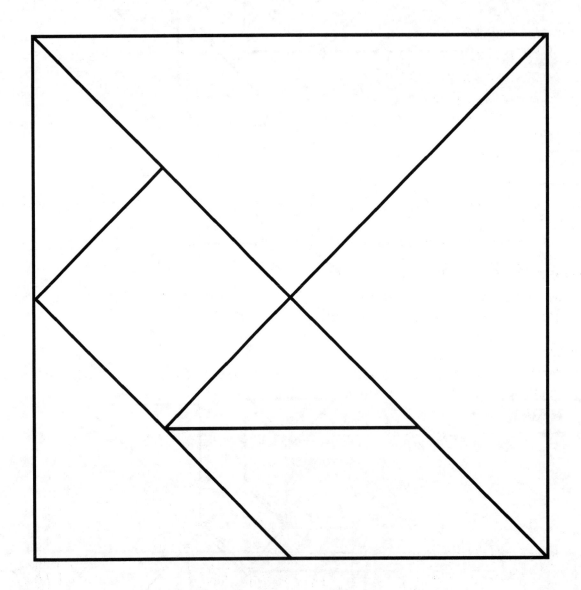

Coding all Species

Question

Can you decode this puzzle to determine the definition below?

Setting the Stage

- Review with students the meanings of *threatened, endangered,* and *extinct.*
- Discuss with students the differences between threats and dangers. Ask them if threats and dangers can be reduced, removed, or reversed. What about extinction?

Materials Needed for Each Individual

- pen or pencil
- black crayon or marker
- data-capture sheet (page 22)

Procedure

1. Have students answer yes or no to each of the ten statements.
2. Have students circle each of the correct answers.
3. When students are finished, the letters circled should spell the missing word in the definition below.

   Animals whose numbers are low and could someday become extinct are called_____.

Extension

Have students create their own codes relating to endangered species and allow them to stump their friends as they attempt to decode the puzzle.

Closure

Discuss what the mysterious word means. Then in their endangered species journals, have students write the definition and draw some examples.

Coding All Species *(cont.)*

If a statement is true, circle the letter in the **YES** column. If false, circle the letter in the **NO** column.

> Animals whose numbers are low and could someday become extinct are_____.

		YES	NO
1. Rhinos are mainly hunted for their fur.	1	B	E
2. Elephants are hunted for their tusks.	2	N	S
3. Camouflage is a survival skill for some species	3	D	R
4. Some species nearly always travel in groups.	4	A	L
5. Our observations are useless when we study science.	5	M	N
6. Animals are the only living creatures on earth.	6	W	G
7. Hawks and tigers are high on nature's food chain.	7	E	P
8. Squirrels and rabbits are predators.	8	E	R
9. Dinosaurs just recently became extinct.	9	K	E
10. Some dinosaurs were predators.	10	D	S

Just the Facts

Natural Causes

For 160 million years the great dinosaurs ruled and roamed our earth along with the saber-toothed cat, the wooly mammoth and millions of other plants and animals that have now become extinct. The dinosaurs became extinct about 65 million years ago, leaving us with few clues to explain their disappearance. Consequently, we are left with many unanswered questions.

Was the extinction of the dinosaurs caused by a sudden catastrophic event such as a gigantic meteorite striking the earth, its dust blocking the sun for months, killing off the food supply? Or could it have been a gradual change in the weather over a 10 million-year span during which the weather got colder, and the dinosaurs, unable to adapt to the change, slowly died off?

Today, hundreds of scientists are trying to solve this great mystery.

Human Causes

Today, humans have managed to speed up extinction of plants and animals at the rate of approximately one species every 60 minutes. The reasons for this increased extinction are many and varied. Modern day extinction is caused by destroying plant and animal habitats, overkilling and hunting, overpopulation, pesticides, pollution, and wasteful habits, among other things. If left unchecked, these practices are so numerous and widespread that they might destroy this unique, beautiful planet. Wildlife, however, has always been tough and will bounce back with a little bit of help now that humankind has finally awakened and opened their eyes to the situation they have created. We are beginning to see that everything is connected, interwoven—and that we should not interfere with the delicate balance of nature.

Yucky Water

Question

What happens to water plants when their homes or habitats become "yucky?"

Setting the Stage

- Define for your students the word *pollution* as unwanted dissolved or solid material found in water.
- Discuss with students that, unfortunately, most people do not know that they must become more water-literate if present and future water problems have any chance of getting solved. For children, these understandings can begin simply by experiencing the fun of water.

Materials Needed for Each Group

- five 1 qt (1 L) containers or five 2-liter clear plastic bottles
- four simulated pollutants—salt, sugar, vinegar, and baking soda
- tap water
- five elodea plants
- labels
- data-capture sheet (page 25), one per student

Note to the teacher: Containers should not contain any bleach or household cleaner. Elodea plants can be purchased in pet stores. They are aquarium plants that grow a few inches (cm) in height and are sold by the bundle. "Pollutants" can be substituted. Use corn starch, saccharine, creamer, flour, etc.

Procedure

1. Fill all five containers about 3/4 full of fresh water. Be sure to label each container (1, 2, 3, 4, and 5).
2. Add 1/2 cup (118 g) of salt to container 1.
3. Add 1/2 cup (118 mL) of vinegar to container 2.
4. Add 1/2 cup (118 g) of sugar to container 3.
5. Add 1/2 cup (118 g) of baking soda to container 4.
6. Tell students that container 5 will contain only fresh water. This is our control group.
7. Have them place an elodea plant in the control container. This should be prepared by the teacher.
8. Call for student volunteers to place elodea leaves in the various containers filled with "pollutants."
9. Over a period of a few weeks, have students record on their data-capture sheets their observations and comparisons.
10. Have students make predictions prior to their daily observations.

Extensions

- Discuss with students the dangers of drinking polluted water and how these pollutants might affect living things in the water, such as fish, frogs, or beavers which build their homes in the water and depend on water for protection.
- Have students list some of the land animals and birds that depend on water for their food.
- Have students make a list of common water pollutants.

Closure

In their endangered species journals, have students write and/or draw what their plants look like after two weeks of testing.

Yucky Water *(cont.)*

Record your observations in the spaces provided.

CUP ONE

CUP THREE

CUP TWO

CUP FOUR

**CUP FIVE
(CONTROL)**

Guess Where I Live?

Question

Do some plant and animal species need a certain climate to live?

Setting the Stage

Discuss with students that many plant and animal species cannot easily move to a new location when their homes or habitats are destroyed. Habitat destruction is the greatest threat facing plant and animal species today. Destroying rain forests, plowing under prairies and grasslands, filling lakes, rivers, filling the air we breathe with pollution, poisons, and pesticides—these are major causes of habitat destruction.

Materials Needed for Each Individual

- pen or pencil
- data-capture sheet (page 27)

Procedure

1. Have students match the animal to its habitat.
2. Then have them relate biome conditions (ecology, characteristic vegetation) to species inhabiting them.

Extensions

- Have students find at least two more animals or plants that live in each one of these habitats.
- Have students illustrate and color their representation of each of these habitats.
- Have students describe why they drew the pictures they did.

Closure

- Discuss, problem solve, and do some critical thinking with students. Pose to students ways people can get the things that they need without disrupting wildlife habitat. Generate classroom lists. For example:
  - ★ Things That Pose Problems:
  - ★ Things That We Need:
  - ★ Alternatives To These Things:
  - ★ Things We Can Do Without:

- Then in their endangered species journals, have students write down these lists.

Guess Where I Live? *(cont.)*

Match the endangered species to its habitat.

____1. LION		a. STREAM
____2. DOLPHIN		b. TROPICAL RAIN FOREST
____3. CACTUS		c. AFRICAN GRASSLAND
____4. ALLIGATOR		d. PRAIRIE
____5. POLAR BEAR		e. OCEAN
____6. PENGUINS		f. DESERT
____7. BIGHORN SHEEP		g. CORAL REEF
____8. CARIBOU/WOLVES		h. RIVER
____9. TROPICAL FISH		i. ANTARTICA
___10. WHOOPING CRANE		j. TUNDRA
___11. BROOK TROUT		k. ARCTIC
___12. BALD EAGLE		l. SWAMP
___13. MONKEY		m. MARSH
___14. WATER FROGS		n. MOUNTAIN RIDGE

Answer Key: 1. c 2. e 3. f 4. l 5. k 6. i 7. n 8. j 9. g 10. l,m
11. a   12. d,f,j,n 13. b 14. h

Tips on Trees

Question

Why are our rain forests disappearing?

Setting the Stage

- Rain forest trees are different from most trees because they grow hundreds of feet (meters) tall with shallow roots and slender trunks. In order to support their weight and height, rain forest trees grow wide bases called buttresses or stilts.
- Tell students that each year more and more of our rain forests are disappearing for a variety of reasons.
- People who live near the rain forest have to cut down trees to make room for farms so they can grow enough food to survive.
- People rely on the wood from rain forests for warming homes, cooking food, and building shelters.
- Trees are cut down by lumber companies which sell the timber to other countries.
- Share with students that destroying a single tree in the rain forest can result in destroying the homes of hundreds of species.

Materials Needed for Each Group

- box of Q-tips
- construction paper
- glue
- transparent tape
- data-capture sheet (page 29), one per student

Note to the teacher: Marshmallows and dry spaghetti or clay and pick-up-sticks can be substituted in this activity.

Procedure

1. Distribute to each group the necessary supplies.
2. Explain to them that they will be given so much time to work as a collaborative group to build a tall, buttressing tree.
3. Have students look at their data-capture sheets for diagrams and questions.

Extensions

- Discuss with the class the effects gravity has on a tall structure. Include discussions of how stability, extreme weather, earthquakes, etc., may affect the structure.
- Have another contest for students involving the construction of bridges using toothpicks and glue. Test their stability by suspending weights from strings attached to each structure. Determine which are stronger and why.

Closure

In their endangered species journals, have students describe the many ways trees are important in our lives and have them brainstorm how to save our rain forests.

Tips on Trees *(cont.)*

Draw your structures and answer the questions.

SAMPLE STRUCTURE 1 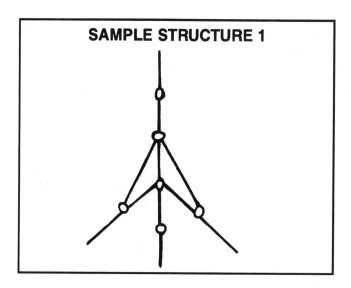	**SAMPLE STRUCTURE 2** 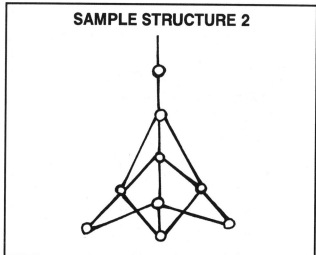
GROUP ATTEMPT 1 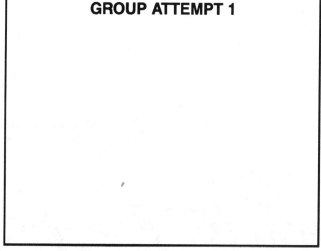	**GROUP ATTEMPT 2**

Describe why your structure is weak or strong. What did you do?

_____

_____

_____

_____

Adding It Up

Question

Why does overhunting cause some animal species to become endangered?

Setting the Stage

Discuss with students that two of the most endangered species on the planet are rhinoceroses and African elephants. Both of these animals have been and still are hunted for their horns and tusks.

Materials Needed for Each Individual

- colored crayons or markers
- data-capture sheet (page 31)

Procedure

1. Have students color in on their data-capture sheets all spaces that add to the numbers 7 or 11.
2. Tell students if added correctly the picture will resemble an endangered species.

Extensions

- Have students research other animal species that have become either threatened, endangered, or extinct because of overkilling.
- Provide students with another endangered species picture pattern.
- Have students create their own puzzles to stump their classmates.

Closure

In their endangered species journals, have students write a story about an endangered species and draw a picture to illustrate it.

Adding It Up (cont.)

Color in all spaces that add up to the numbers 7 or 11.

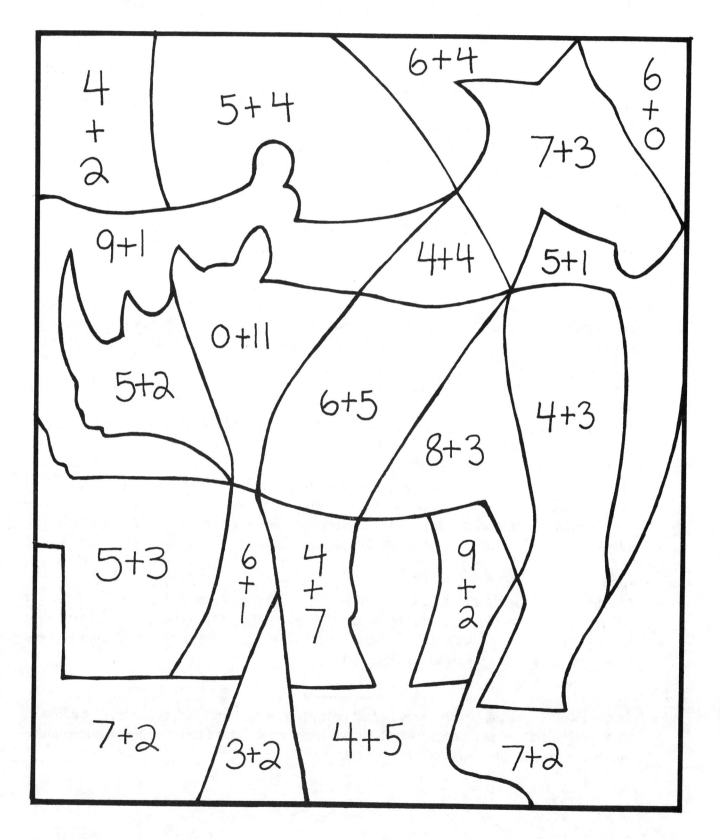

A Dwindling Classroom Habitat

Question

How would you feel if your space were invaded and there was not much room left to move around, play, or be comfortable?

Setting the Stage

- Discuss with students that as the population of humankind gets bigger, the need increases for places to live. For every person born, there must be a place to live, to go to school, to play, and to visit.

- Discuss with students that as the population increases, the need also increases for more products made from wood, more land for growing food, and more area for roads and cities.

Materials Needed for Each Group

- masking tape or string
- yard or meter stick
- data-capture sheet (page 33), one per student

Procedure

1. Have students describe on their data-capture sheets their classroom environment as if it were their habitat. Have them include a description of how they get around in the classroom, how much privacy or space they or their group has, how much play space is available, etc.

2. Now, have the groups measure the dimensions of the classroom and record the number of students occupying this space.

3. Have them mark off the room dimensions in quarters using masking tape or string. For instance, if a classroom is 12 yds x 12 yds (12 m x 12 m), then your quarters would each be 6 yds x 6 yds (6 m x 6 m). (See diagram page 33.)

4. Have students describe these same things listed in number one when the whole class is restricted in the confines of 3/4 of the classroom, 1/2 of the classroom, and 1/4 of the classroom. Requiring the same number of individuals to occupy progressively less and less space should yield some very interesting descriptions on students' data-capture sheets.

Extension

Distribute equal shares of M & M's® to your students. Explain to them that this is their food rationing. With dwindling habitats and increased numbers, there will be less food. Find out what happens when the candy has to be split among twice as many of them or how much each will get if there is only half the supply available next time.

Closure

Discuss with your class how and why habitat destruction leads to the endangerment of wildlife. Then in their endangered species journals, have students write down their feelings about wildlife endangerment and share some of their thoughts with the class.

A Dwindling Classroom Habitat *(cont.)*

Fill in the information needed. Use the back or a second sheet of paper if necessary.

1. Describe your classroom habitat. Include such things as play space, privacy, stretching room, and study space.

12 yds (m)

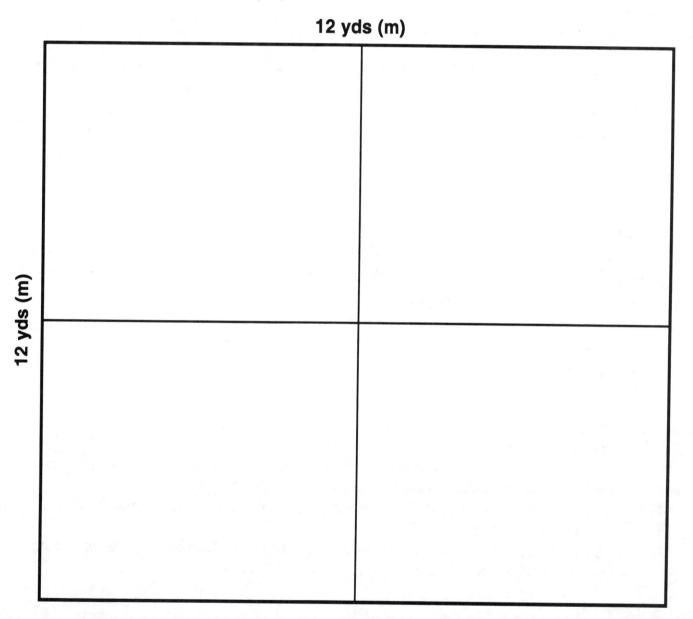

12 yds (m)

2. Describe your classroom habitat if your class is restricted to 3/4 of the room.

3. Describe your classroom habitat if your class is restricted to 1/2 of the room.

4. Describe your classroom habitat if your class is restricted to 1/4 of the room.

Beak Coordination: Which Beaks Have It?

Question

Is there evidence that suggests that birds or other animals have adapted throughout time in order to survive?

Setting the Stage

- Have students cut out illustrations of many types of bird species. Discuss with students ways that birds have adapted to changes in their environment as a means of coping with habitat destruction, natural predators, dwindling food supplies, and severe weather conditions. Point out to students that there are many sizes and shapes of beaks found on different species of birds.
- Have students classify the many shared illustrations by the type of beak the bird has.
- Brainstorm with the class the function and mechanics of the various beak types. For instance, does the food source of a particular bird depend highly on its beak design? How about where it lives and nests? Explain.

Materials Needed for Each Group

- yarn
- marbles
- popcorn
- pennies
- toothpicks
- peanuts (shelled)
- tweezers
- student scissors
- clothespins
- drinking straws or pencils (unsharpened)
- stopwatch or clock (with second hand)
- plastic spoons
- data-capture sheet (page 35), one per student

Procedure

1. Distribute data-capture sheets and containers with enough of each of the materials for students to complete their experience.
2. Explain to the class that certain objects represent a certain type of beak design and that other objects represent the foods that can be manipulated by a particular beak.
3. Have all students in a group predict and test themselves by using various functional tools as beaks for picking up various food sources.
4. The other group members will be responsible for keeping time. Each object representing food should be tested by each of the objects representing the beaks for one minute.

Extensions

- Ask students if they think there are other adaptations by birds. For example, their feet seem designed for grabbing or perching, and their wings seem designed for aerodynamics. Explain.
- Have students choose a bird to research.

Closure

In their endangered species journals, have students describe how some beaks are better suited than others for eating certain foods.

Beak Coordination: Which Beaks Have It? *(cont.)*

Record the number or amount of each food source you were able to pick up in one minute, using each of the beak types.

food → beak type ↓	peanuts (grubs)	marbles (snails)	yarn or strings (worms)	pennies (beetles)	toothpicks (caterpillars)
tweezers					
scissors					
straws					
clothespin					
plastic spoons					

 #628 Endangered Species—Primary

How Big Is Big?

Questions

Can you imagine how big some of the dinosaurs were? Do you think that their size contributed to their extinction?

Setting the Stage

- Discuss with students that many dinosaurs roamed the earth millions of years ago. However, they are now extinct. Scientists hold many different views as to why the dinosaurs did not succeed. Some scientists believe that there were major catastrophes such as earthquakes and volcanoes that destroyed their habitats and food supplies. Other scientists believe that meteorites hit the earth creating great dust clouds, blocking out the sunlight and making the environment cold.
- Tell students that this activity will give them an idea of just how difficult it was for dinosaurs to move around, find food, and seek adequate shelter.

Materials Needed for Each Group

- string
- wooden sticks (markers)
- yard or meter stick
- dinosaur dimensions
- open space

Procedure

1. Begin by telling students how big some dinosaurs were. Have them describe how big this really was by comparing it to things they know, like a car or house.
2. Take the class out to the playground or any open area where they can measure the length and width of a dinosaur as if it were lying on its side in front of them.
3. Have the students measure in yards (meters) the dimensions you provide them with. They should mark their measurements with a wooden stick or any object which they can run string around to outline their completed dimensions.
4. Assign different groups a different dinosaur and its corresponding dimensions. This way they can compare later.
5. Once the dimension outlines are completed, find out just how many students in the class, or how many classes in the school, can fit inside the stringed outlines. This should provide a good understanding of "How big is big?"

Extensions

- Have students outline the dimensions of fern trees that existed long ago so they can compare them to what we typically think of as a fern today.
- Have students compare modern day giants such as whales and elephants with the dinosaurs.

Closure

In their endangered species journals, have students record their observations and draw their dinosaurs. They should label them and compare its size to others they viewed outside where the activity took place.

Fishy Manipulative

Question

What would you do if you were in this situation?

Setting the Stage

- Tell students that over time many species adapt or learn new behaviors to accommodate their new or changing environments. This is necessary for many species if they are going to continue to survive. For example, many species have well-developed senses that help them to hear, smell, or see their oncoming predators. Others can move swiftly and at all times remain alert.

- Ask students what would they do if they were fish and a large predator such as a shark or octopus were heading right for them?

Materials Needed for Each Individual

- eight drinking straws, toothpicks, or pick-up sticks
- a flat table surface
- fish diagram (page 38)

Procedure

1. Using eight straws, toothpicks, or pick-up-sticks, have students produce the pattern of a fish. (See diagram page 38)
2. Next, have them manipulate the pattern so that it becomes an identical fish swimming in the opposite direction. The trick is to make only three moves.
3. To make the fish point upward (to get food) and downward (to seek shelter), students will need to make two moves.

Extensions

- Have students follow similar procedures but this time create a pattern so a fish is swimming on either side (90 degrees) from where it initially was. (They can make only two moves.)
- This trick is really fishy, so don't let it get them down. If they get frustrated they are sure to sink.

Closure

In their endangered species journals, have students draw diagrams showing how the fish directions were changed.

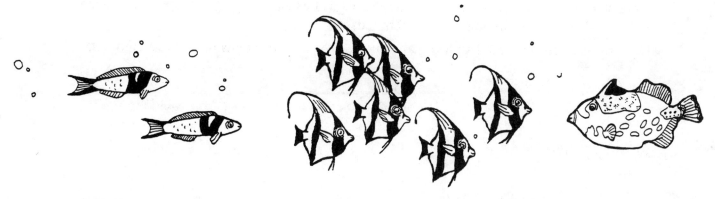

Fishy Manipulative (cont.)

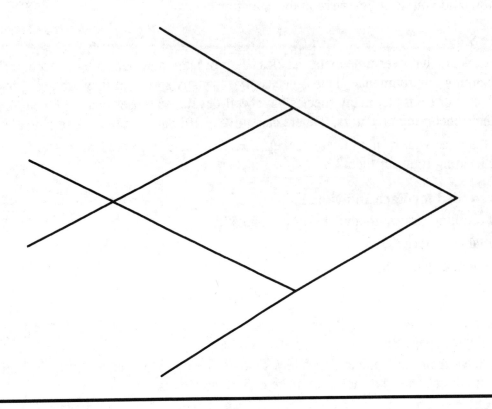

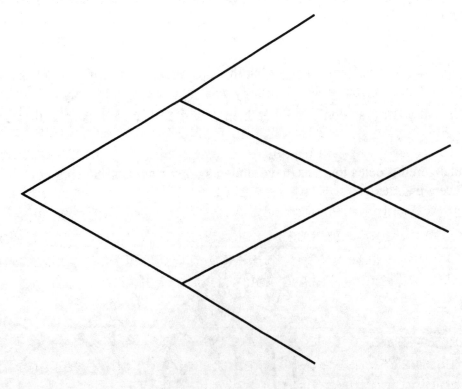

38

Just the Facts

Plants and animals deserve our respect and gratitude. Humankind could not exist without them. Forests provide us with lumber to build houses and furniture. The paper we are writing on is made with cellulose from trees. Cellulose is also used in making carpets, clothing, toothbrush handles, ping pong balls, buttons, eyeglass frames, salad dressing, and luggage. The sap of trees can be used in making coating for pills, cosmetics, mouthwash, perfumes, soap, and syrup. We eat the fruit, nuts, roots, and bark of many trees. Most importantly, forests provide oxygen for us to breathe.

Forests also provide homes and food for wildlife, act as "water filters" and prevent soil erosion. Nevertheless, millions of trees are being cut down every year. If our rain forests vanish, so will millions of plant and animal species, consequently creating havoc with our weather patterns around the world. There will be no more foxglove plant to produce digitalis—a heart drug that cannot be made synthetically—or other drugs that wild plants provide us with. Remember that plants have also provided us with food, mainly the big seven—potatoes, barley, wheat, rice, corn, sweet potato, and cassava. Plants and animals also serve as food for other plants and animals. Each creature or plant plays a vital role in our existence because everything is connected and dependent on one another. This is why we call the earth and its various regions ecosystems.

Deforestation has decreased transpiration (water vapor released into the atmosphere by plants and trees) which has interfered with the water cycle and may cause severe consequences to global climatic conditions. Deforestation decreases the amount of oxygen released into our atmosphere, thereby raising the carbon dioxide levels and promoting global warming, a dangerous possibility.

All plants and animals play an essential role in the overall balance of nature. If we fail to preserve them, we risk adverse effects on ourselves and the world we live in. By helping them, we help ourselves!

Food Chain Mobile

Question

Is the disruption of nature's food chains upsetting our balanced ecological systems?

Setting the Stage

- Tell students a *biome* refers to a geographical location that is characteristic of specific climatic conditions. These climatic conditions have determined the plant and animal species adapted to thrive in a given biome. Through time, nature has established balances and harmony among the organisms existing within a given biome.
- Review with students the different biomes of the world and the plants and animals that populate them.
- Review with students some common food chains in your region. Have students come up with some examples.

Materials Needed for Each Group

- description of biomes (pages 42-44), one each per student
- pictures, photos, and illustrations of plants and animals
- drinking straws
- string
- transparent tape
- scissors
- tagboard or sturdy construction paper

Note to the teacher: In this activity students will work together to create products that illustrate various food chains of the earth's natural biomes.

Procedure

1. Instruct student groups to select a biome and to cut out or draw pictures of plants or animals indigenous to that biome. Note: Indicate to students the need for magazines, postcards, and other illustrations for this activity a few days prior so that they can collect them.
2. Student group illustrations should include three carnivores, three herbivores, three plants, and three figures representing physical or earth science—for example, sun, moon, planets, clouds, stars, earth, etc.
3. Have students make two long straws by attaching several straws together. Instruct students to pinch ends together and tape so they will not slip apart.
4. Next, have students tape or tie straws together diagonally.
5. Then, have students punch a small hole toward the top of each plant or animal picture that they have glued to the tagboard.
6. Next, have students attach a string to each of the pictures at varied lengths. Have them use 32" (80 cm) length for sun, stars, etc. Have them use 24" (60 cm) length for producers (plants— low on the food pyramid). Have them use 16" (40 cm) length for herbivores (plant-eating consumers). Finally, have them use 8" (20 cm) length for carnivores (meat eaters).

Food Chain Mobile *(cont.)*

7. Then, have students attach each string to one end of a straw and repeat with all the illustrations. Tell them there should be one picture at the end of each straw.

8. Finally, have students attach the various straws to the mobile to form a food chain design to hang in the classroom.

Extensions

- Reinforce to students how a food chain or pyramid begins with the lower links or triangle base composed of producers, which make up a greater variety and percentage of the whole. This level is followed by herbivorous organisms such as insects and rodents. The last links or the highest level is composed of the consumers, which are carnivorous organisms.

- Have students extend their research of food chains to more complicated producer-consumer networks, such as food pyramids and/or food webs. This can be accomplished by assigning a consumer that preys on more than a single organism and has more than a single predator, such as a squirrel. A squirrel feeds on a variety of nuts, roots, and plants. He is appealing to canines, felines, and man as food or for sport. Therefore, the squirrel makes an ideal specimen for the center of a food web where he is part of several different food chains within a single food web.

Closure

In their endangered species journals, have students investigate examples of food chains that are in trouble in the biome you live in. Then answer the following question, How do these problems compare to the problems of food chains in other biomes?

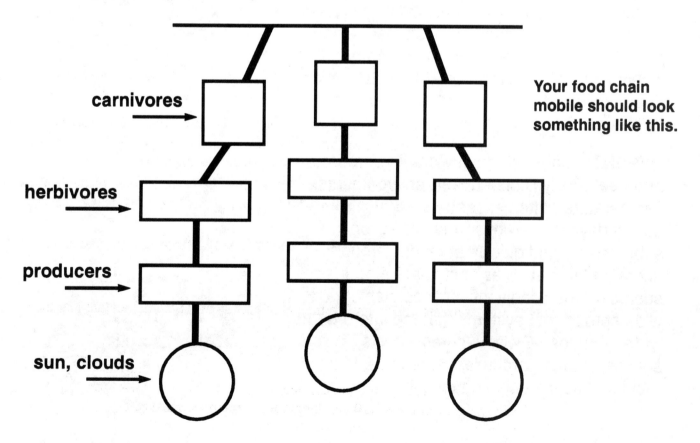

carnivores →

herbivores →

producers →

sun, clouds →

Your food chain mobile should look something like this.

 #628 Endangered Species—Primary

Food Chain Mobile *(cont.)*

A biome refers to a geographic location of "life" on the earth's land or water that is characterized by weather conditions, such as amount of rain, sunlight, humidity and/or temperature. The specific weather of a biome determines what kinds of plants or animals can survive there. Biomes of the land include coniferous, deciduous, and tropical rain forest, desert, grassland, and tundra. Water biomes are classified as fresh water or marine.

CONIFEROUS FOREST: Cone-bearing plants that thrive in cold winters exist in this biome. Conifers make up approximately 30% of the world's forests. Bears, elk, deer, moose, lynx, porcupines, squirrels, and many varieties of insects inhabit coniferous forests.

DECIDUOUS FOREST: Moderate temperature and rain are characteristic of this biome. A variety of broad-leaved trees that lose their leaves annually, such as maple, oak, beech, and hickory form the canopy of these forests. The understory (a slightly lower layer of trees) is formed by birch, aspen and pine trees, which are inhabited by many insects and birds. Raccoons, opossum, mice, deer, snakes, and insects inhabit deciduous forests.

DESERT: Long periods of extreme dryness and heat are typical of desert environments. Temperatures often exceed 100˚ (38˚ C) during daylight; however, they can drop substantially and quickly at night. Drought-tolerant plants such as cactus are adapted to such extreme conditions. These plants have wide-spread root systems that tap into ground water sources. Owls, vultures, hawks, snakes, lizards, tarantulas, scorpions, foxes, rabbits, bats, camels and mice inhabit deserts.

Food Chain Mobile *(cont.)*

GRASSLAND: Characterized by large, open areas of land, these biomes are covered by rich, grasses. Typically, summers are warm and winters are cool. Grasslands are located on all five continents of the world. These areas are too moist to have become deserts and not rich enough to have developed into forests. Zebras, prairie dogs, mice, coyotes, and kangaroos occupy grasslands.

TROPICAL RAIN FOREST: Wet, warm, and humid conditions are common in this biome. Broad-leaved evergreens, ferns, and orchids are home to tropical rain forests. It is thought that in these areas there exist many species of plants not yet discovered by humans. A tropical rain forest is layered by the plants occupying its space. The canopy level is usually so dense that very little sunlight can penetrate through to the lower levels. Therefore, shrubbery is not common; instead, the forest floor is occupied by fungi and mosses. Monkeys and many exotic birds such as parrots live in the canopies of tropical rain forests. At lower levels, species of insects such as butterflies are abundant. Various species of snakes, lizards, and other reptiles are common. Eagles, jaguars, and leopards are predators to small game of the tropical rain forests. Only 7% of the earth's land surface is rain forest, but it is estimated that 45,600-55,200 sq. mi. (118,104-142,968 sq. km.) of rain forest are destroyed each year.

TUNDRA: Mostly cold and dry conditions characterize this biome. Days go by between sunsets in summer, and in winter a few hours of daylight is typical. Plants grow close to the ground where temperatures are warmest and protection from the frigid winds is greatest. These typically include mosses, lichens, and short flowering plants. Many birds such as fowl, geese, ducks, and gulls nest in the low-lying vegetation. As winter approaches, it is these birds that migrate south. Caribou, polar bears, hares, foxes, wolves, and owls are inhabitants of tundra regions.

Food Chain Mobile *(cont.)*

FRESH WATER: Freshwater biomes are contained in streams and rivers (running water sources) and lakes and ponds (still water sources). Algae and freshwater plants anchor to rocks and pebbles as an adaptation to water currents. Insect larvae inhabit this location by grasping plants with their hooks or suckers. Where freshwater flow is slow, many plants occupy river or stream banks. Snails, crayfish, and bass are some of the organisms making up the living communities existing there. In lakes and ponds where freshwater is very still, rooted plants are common. Plankton and algae are bountiful, often blocking sunlight from lower depths. Worms, bacteria, and fungi exist in deep, dark regions near the water's bottom. Insects (dragonflies, mosquitoes, and gnats), frogs, fish, birds, and snakes inhabit shores of fresh water biomes.

MARINE: Oceans of the world make up 70% of the earth's surface, containing the greatest variety of species and considered the largest biome of the earth. Marine biomes are divided into zones characterized by conditions that dictate the forms of life occupying a region. Coasts are located in the littoral zone (areas affected by tides and interfacing with beaches). This shallow zone includes tide-pool organisms (seastars, kelp, and crabs) adaptive to wet and dry conditions. These organisms cling to rocks or burrow in sand. The sublittoral zone extends beyond the continental shelf and is populated by protozoa and algae due to rich nutrients and ideal sunlight exposure. Seals, squids, and turtles are consumers of food webs existing here. The pelagic zone comprises the deeper, darker marine regions. Food is scarce, and conditions are governed by lack of light and water pressure. Bacteria thrive on sea floors. Food chains consist of small fish, predator fish, sharks, and rays. Also, marine mammals (whales and dolphins) inhabit marine biomes.

Food Chain Mobile *(cont.)*

Biomes of the World

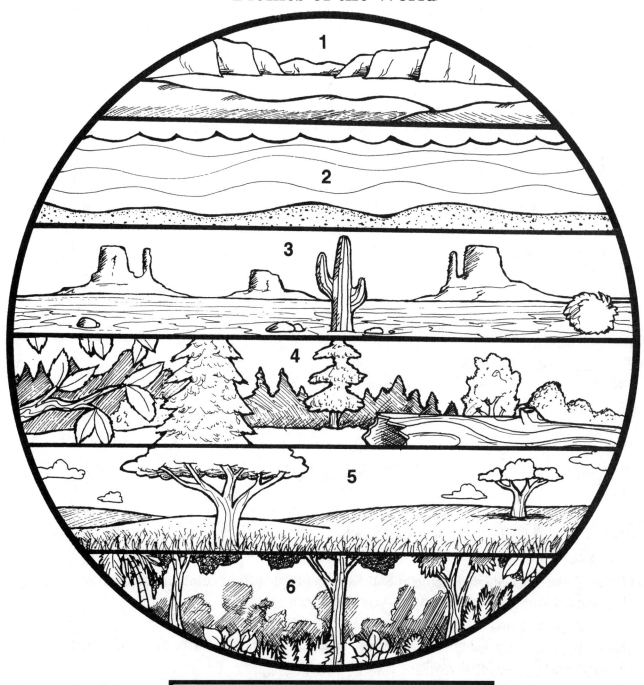

1. Tundra
2. Freshwater/Marine
3. Desert
4. Coniferous/Decidous Forest
5. Grassland
6. Tropical Rain Forest

Nature's Missing Links

Questions

Does altering a food chain or food web threaten ecosystems of the earth? Can the disruption of a single food chain alter other food chains of the same web?

Setting the Stage

- Tell students a food chain is a series of living things directly linked to one another by what they eat. A plant is always the first link in a food chain. Plants are considered producers because they rely upon the sun's rays for photosynthesis. This is the process by which plants gain energy to produce their own food. Consumers follow producers on a food chain. Consumers are those organisms that must rely on plants or animals in their environment for food. Herbivores (plant-eating animals) and carnivores (meat-eating animals) are each consumers. Herbivores make ideal prey for many carnivorous predator animals. Therefore, they follow producers on the food chain.

- The sap of the pine tree is sucked by tiny plant lice. Spiders eat the lice. Small birds eat the spiders and the lice, and hawks prey on the small birds. The hawk is the top carnivore, the last link in the food chain.

- Discuss with students several examples of food chains and food webs. Using your example of a food web, discuss with the class how it is composed of several individual food chains. Ask students how many food chains they can locate.

Materials Needed for Each Group

- pictures and illustrations of plants and animals
- scissors
- glue stick
- poster paper
- index cards
- string
- single-hole punch

Procedure

1. Review with students the biomes of the world—fresh water, marine, coniferous, deciduous, and tropical forests, deserts, grassland, and tundra.
2. Have students make a list of known plants and animals of a given biome.
3. Allow students to cut out pictures from magazines, to draw and write about the plants and animals of their chosen biome.
4. Have students create food chains to represent their particular biomes on poster paper.
5. If classroom understanding is apparent, have students proceed by creating an elaborate food web using food chains they have discovered.
6. Ask students what happens when a single organism of a food chain disappears or is introduced.
7. Ask students what happens to other food chains within the food web of the above altered food chain. Explain.

Nature's Missing Links *(cont.)*

Extensions

- Have students punch holes at the top and bottom of their index cards. They should be holding the cards vertically. Instruct them to glue or draw a picture of plants and animals of a given food chain on each index card. Then have them link the index cards together using string or yarn. Producers should be represented on the first card (bottom) and consumers towards the last card (top).

- Have students describe the environment of each of the world's biomes and list several species indigenous to that particular biome.

Closure

In their endangered species journals, have students list several animal groups by what they eat. Be sure that they have included the following terms: carnivores, herbivores, decomposers, producers, and consumers. Then, pose the following question: In what ways have humans disrupted food chains?

Power of Nature

Question

Can natural events take care of cleansing the earth's water supply?

Setting the Stage

Discuss with students nature's fascinating water cycle: water evaporates, forms clouds, condenses, and forms rain over and over again on our planet. It is this process that cleans the water and purifies it through a great recycling process. However, natural cleansing can only take care of so much pollution at one time. It cannot keep up with all of the pollution generated by factories, cars, and litter.

Materials Needed for Each Group

- sealable plastic bags
- small transparent cups
- water
- food coloring
- data-capture sheet (page 49), one per student

Procedure

1. Have student groups prepare samples of polluted water. In this case, water mixed with a couple of drops of food coloring will be considered polluted.
2. Have students fill the cup part way with water and have them add the food coloring. Tell them not much is needed; a little goes a long way.
3. Have students place the plastic container filled with their polluted water into a plastic bag. Help them seal it securely.
4. Have students tape or suspend the bags from a window sill or a designated spot outside in the sunlight. You may want students to vary locations with variables such as temperature, light, etc., for comparison and higher-order thinking later.
5. Have students observe closely. The water will soon begin to evaporate and separate from the polluted mixture. Clear condensation will begin to form on the bags.
6. Have students record observations and illustrate this experience on their data-capture sheets.
7. Explain to students that the warm sun is absorbed by the water and it begins to turn into vapor. This water vapor is very light and floats away from the polluted or colored mixture. As it cools in the surrounding baggie, it will begin to condense and form a clean liquid once again.

Extensions

Have students include time and temperature as a measurable observation in this experience.

Closure

Relate the concepts of evaporation and condensation to students' lives. For instance, when a tea kettle boils from the heat of a burner, gas or water vapor can be observed. Also, when clouds travel over cooler land surfaces, the gas or water vapor begins to cool and the clouds will condense (squeeze together). This eventually creates a liquid heavier than air—rain. In their endangered species journals, have students illustrate a scene incorporating all of these concepts.

Power of Nature *(cont.)*

Fill in the information needed.

Draw the polluted water.

Color the polluted water.

Draw your observations.

Comments about your experience:

_____

_____

_____

Pollution Diffusion Disaster

Question

Can we prevent damage to bird eggs by controlling unnatural oil spills in water?

Setting the Stage

Tell students that throughout the last few hundred years humans have depended upon oil for heating and industry. The extraction and transportation of oil has resulted in serious environmental consequences as a result of drilling, accidental spills, and pollution from its use. For instance, the Exxon Valdez spill was responsible for much wildlife destruction. Several aquatic and shoreline habitats were destroyed and food chains disrupted. Otters, many species of birds and fish, and several varieties of flora fall victim to such accidents every year.

Materials Needed for Each Group

- plastic dish containers or mixing bowls
- hard-boiled eggs
- food coloring
- vegetable oil
- stopwatch or clock (with second hand)
- plastic knife
- data-capture sheet (page 51), one per student

Procedure

1. Distribute to groups 3-5 hard-boiled eggs, 8-16 oz (250-500 mL) of vegetable oil, food coloring (in a dropper bottle), and a bowl or container to perform the experience.
2. Have students place a large paper towel directly under the plastic container.
3. Then, have students mix thoroughly the vegetable oil and a few drops of food coloring. On their data-capture sheets, have them describe how this mixture reacts and appears.
4. Instruct students to place the number of eggs they are to test into the mixture and have them remove one egg at a time at five-minute intervals. Then on their data-capture sheets, record any external observations of the eggs they remove.
5. Instruct students that as each individual egg is removed they are to shell it and slice it open. Then on their data-capture sheets, record any internal observations made.

Extensions

- Using three plastic cups, have students fill each respectively with 8 oz (250 mL) of the following liquids—oil, water, and corn syrup. Add blue food coloring to the water and red food coloring to the corn syrup. Ask students to predict the order arranged by pouring each cup individually into a large clear cylinder. Have them record the masses of each, volumes of each. Which sinks to the bottom? Which liquid floats on top? Did any liquids mix together? Why?
- Reinforce to students the concept of *density*, a property of matter used to describe the amount of matter occupying a given volume.

Closure

In their endangered species journals, have students write about their reactions to off-shore drilling, past spills, or other environmental accidents.

Pollution Diffusion Disaster *(cont.)*

Answer the questions and record your observations on the chart.

Describe the mixture of the vegetable oil and food coloring._____

_____

_____

_____

	EXTERNAL OBSERVATION	INTERNAL OBSERVATION
EGG 1 **(5 min.)**		
EGG 2 **(10 min.)**		
EGG 3 **(15 min.)**		
EGG 4 **(20 min.)**		
EGG 5 **(25 min.)**		

     #628 Endangered Species—Primary

Recycling—Mathematically Profitable

Question

Can preserving nature by recycling be profitable?

Setting the Stage

Tell students that to recycle many materials is to help preserve our environment, to help prevent the endangerment of wildlife, and to be profitable all at the same time. Glass, aluminum, plastic, paper, and styrofoam are materials we can recycle, yet we continue to throw them away.

Materials Needed for Each Group

- three large bins
- three labels: Aluminum Cans, Plastic Bottles, and Glass Bottles
- one box of large paper clips
- data-capture sheets (pages 53-54), one each per student

Procedure

1. Have your class collect aluminum cans, plastic two-liter bottles, and glass bottles for four consecutive weeks.
2. Have student groups identify a location and label a bin for each of the materials collected.
3. Have them find out the redemption value for each of the items.
4. At the end of each week, have students categorize, count, and weigh each of the like materials. For example, categorize or classify by brand name, color, size, etc.
5. Have them determine the value of their combined collections by multiplying the numbers of each by the redemption value of each.
6. Have students record this information weekly on their data-capture sheets.
7. At the end of the activity, have students transfer their weekly totals data to their data-capture sheets with the class totals and calculate the total amount earned by the class.

Extensions

- Have students add up the sums of each material after the four-week allotment of time and determine averages, means, etc.
- Have students hang three equal-sized but different-colored strings from the board or wall. Have them identify each string as aluminum, plastic, or glass. Using their total numbers collected over the four weeks, have them create a classroom graph depicting this data. Explain to students that each paper clip represents ten. For every ten of each item, select volunteers to place a paper clip on the designated string. The number of clips on each of the strings should create a visual representation and comparison of totals.

Closure

In their endangered species journals, have students explain the many advantages of recycling.

Recycling—Mathematically Profitable (cont.)

Fill in the chart with the needed information.

WEEK 1	**CANS**			
	GLASS			
	PLASTIC			
WEEK 2	**CANS**			
	GLASS			
	PLASTIC			
WEEK 3	**CANS**			
	GLASS			
	PLASTIC			
WEEK 4	**CANS**			
	GLASS			
	PLASTIC			

Recycling—Mathematically Profitable *(cont.)*

Fill in the class totals of all recycling and complete the chart.

Number of bottles collected by the class = _____

Number of aluminum cans collected by the class = _____

Number of 2-liter bottles collected by the class = _____

Total Number of Recyclable Goods Collected = _____

Number of glass bottles times redemption rate

_____ X _____ = _____

Number of aluminum cans times redemption rate

_____ X _____ = _____

Number of plastic bottles times redemption rate

_____ X _____ = _____

Total Amount Earned by the Classroom = _____

At Home Conservation

Question

Can we be conditioned to conserve energy and preserve the environment daily?

Setting the Stage

- Discuss with students that there are many things that we all do on a regular basis that contribute greatly to increased pollution—such as not recycling aluminum/plastic/glass, not turning off lights or shutting doors, wasting water, etc.
- Discuss with students that conserving natural resources will benefit us and future generations.

Materials Needed for Each Student

- colored markers or crayons
- data-capture sheet (page 56)

Procedure

1. Send a data-capture sheet home with students each day for an entire week.
2. Tell students that for each box colored in and initialed by a parent or guardian, they will gain a point. There are 25 points possible in all. The coloring key is as follows:

    Turning off lights - yellow

    Conserving water - blue

    Shutting doors - black

    Lawn conservation - green

    Other (explain, e.g., recycling) - red

3. Reward students with high scores with a free homework pass or some other positive reinforcement—perhaps stickers or a conservation or preservation award.

Extension

Investigate with students other ways that people can conserve energy and preserve wildlife at home, school, or anywhere. Have students construct a bar graph to represent those things that contribute the greatest to air pollution, land pollution, and water pollution.

Closure

In their endangered species journals, have students answer the following questions about their conservation experience. What unique approaches were taken? Who really worked hard to make a difference? Are these things that we are doing really going to help?

At Home Conservation *(cont.)*

Dear Parents: Please initial the boxed area for a particular day if your child conserved energy that day, ultimately helping protect the environment.

	MONDAY	TUESDAY	WEDNESDAY	THURSDAY	FRIDAY
TURNING OFF LIGHTS					
SHUTTING DOORS AND WINDOWS					
CONSERVING WATER					
LAWNS AND GARDENS					
OTHER (EXPLAIN!)					

Door Knob Hanging Tree

Question

Can we do things around our own homes to conserve energy and preserve nature?

Setting the Stage

Discuss with students the many things that we take for granted because we are accustomed to modern times. For instance, we never think of meat as actual animals; we think of it as food that we get at the grocery store. But, where does it really come from? We do not think about where the trash goes after we use up products. We simply throw it in the garbage, and then the city comes and picks it up once a week. But, where does it all go then? We think of cooling or heating our homes, but we do not think about the energy being used or the fuel being burned.

Materials Needed for Each Student

- pattern sheet (page 58), one per student
- colored markers or crayons
- scissors

Procedure

1. Distribute the pattern sheet (page 58) to each student. Explain to them that they are going to make a product to help remind them to conserve energy at home.
2. Have students cut out the pattern and color it as instructed.
3. Have students take it home and explain to their families what it is intended for. They should hang it from a door where all can see.

Extension

Have students work in groups to develop a poster depicting some way we can conserve energy and thus preserve wildlife.

Closure

Discuss with the class several examples in which we waste energy and disrupt the environment: 1) fossil fuel–smog 2) plastic containers–nonbiodegradable waste
State several cause-and-effect relationships pertaining to the preservation of our environment:
1) composting–fertile earth 2) ladybugs–aphids
Then in their endangered species journals, have students generate lists of pros and cons and rank each, from most beneficial to greatest harm.

Door Knob Hanging Tree *(cont.)*

Cut out pattern and color.

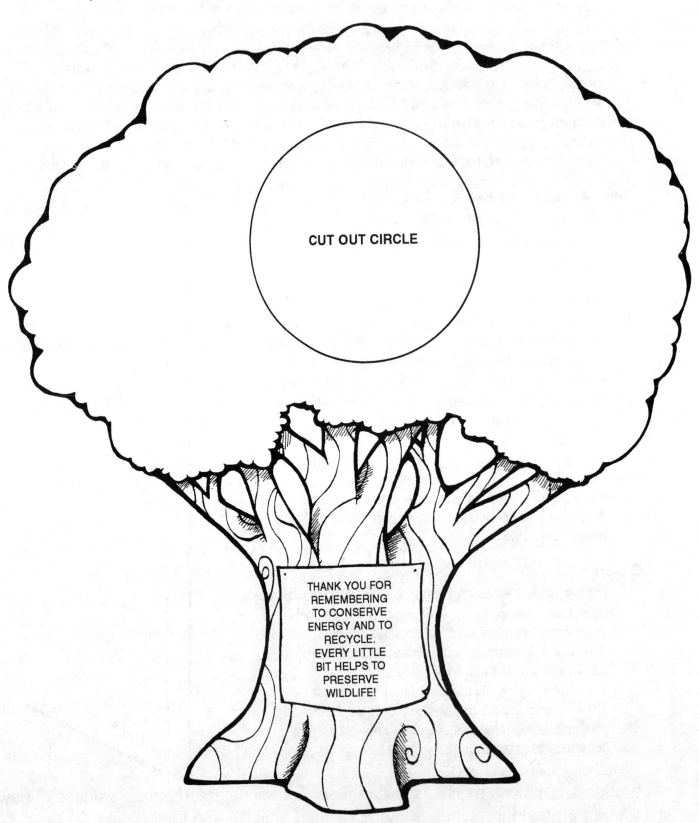

Just the Facts

POSITIVE SCIENCE ATTITUDES:

Teachers and parents can help students develop positive science attitudes by fostering, guiding, and increasing their natural capacity to appreciate, investigate, discover, explore, enjoy, and study the processes of nature. These positive science attitudes must be nurtured and geared to help students develop specific investigative methods of the natural world along with the skills necessary to apply their knowledge for the benefit of others.

THE ACTIONS YOU CAN TAKE:

- Use no products made from threatened or endangered species (like an ivory figurine made from an elephant's tusk). If a product is the result of a habitat being destroyed, do not buy it.

- Throw no garbage into streams nor litter the land.

- Buy no exotic pets, such as parrots or tropical fish, which have been taken from the wild.

- Read, become aware, and understand how living things are dependent on one another.

- Know your facts, share them with friends, and write your government officials.

WHERE TO FIND HELP:

Endangered and threatened species need our help! Government agencies such as the United States Environmental Protection Agency, the United States Department of Agriculture, the United States Fish and Wildlife Services, and the National Park Service, along with State Fish and Wildlife Agencies, and private groups are making available information that will heighten our awareness of how we can protect threatened and endangered species and their habitats.

Lefty and Righty—Not All Right

Question

Can humans set "right" the imbalances of nature which we have "left" for other creatures?

Setting the Stage

- Discuss with your class information pertaining to these mammals—lions and rhinos. Explain where their natural habitats are and what biomes they once had or continue to have.
- Brainstorm with the class various reasons as to why these mammals have become endangered.
- Have students investigate whether or not any other creatures sharing their biomes may have become extinct by natural means.

Materials Needed for Each Individual

drinking straw (varied colors)

Procedure

1. Instruct students to stand up and to form a large circle in the classroom.
2. Distribute a single straw to each student. Different colors should be given to every second or third student.
3. Direct students to listen carefully and to follow directions as you read them a story about "Lefty" the Lion and "Righty" the Rhino.
4. Explain to students that every time the words *right* or *left* come up, they must pass the straw in the appropriate directions.

Extensions

- Have students create their own stories about different threatened or endangered species.
- Have students extend their research about lions and rhinos so that the class may become more knowledgeable on those subjects.

Closure

In their endangered species journals, have students answer the following questions about their experience. Was it difficult to follow directions? Did the mistake of one affect all? What do you think about "Lefty's" and "Righty's" situation? Would you like to help?

Lefty and Righty—Not All Right (cont.)

IS IT RIGHT THAT TODAY MANY SPECIES OF PLANTS AND ANIMALS ARE ENDANGERED? IN SOME CASES THERE ARE ALMOST NONE LEFT.

"LEFTY" THE LION AND "RIGHTY" THE RHINO, FOR INSTANCE, HAVE MUCH LESS HABITAT LEFT, HABITAT WHICH THEY ONCE RIGHTFULLY OCCUPIED. YOU SEE, A COUPLE OF CENTURIES AGO PEOPLE LEFT MANY PORTS TO COME TO AMERICA. THEY ALSO LEFT FOR EXOTIC PLACES TO DEMONSTRATE THEIR RIGHT TO TRAP AND HUNT ANIMALS FOR EXHIBIT, SPORT, OR PRODUCT.

AS HUMANS REQUIRED MORE SPACE TO EXIST, THEY ASSUMED THE RIGHT TO CLAIM MORE AND MORE TERRITORY. DWINDLING HABITATS AND COMPETITION WITH HUMANS FOR FOOD FOUND "LEFTY" THE LION NOT FEELING ALL RIGHT. THIS, AS WELL AS HUMANS' "SUPERIORITY" TO AND/OR FEAR OF "LEFTY" THE LION, LEFT LITTLE ALTERNATIVE OTHER THAN TO FLEE RIGHT AWAY. THIS LEFT NATURE'S BALANCE SOMEWHAT OTHER THAN RIGHT.

MEANWHILE, WITH A TUSK POINTED UPRIGHT AND HIS HEAD TURNED LEFT, A RHINO NAMED "RIGHTY" BECAME ALERTED TO SOME NOW FAMILIAR SOUNDS. THEY WERE THE SOUNDS OF GUN SHOTS AS BULLETS LEFT THE BARREL OF A RIFLE INVENTED BY HUMANS. "RIGHTY" WAS AWARE THAT HUMANS WERE RIGHT BEHIND AND CLOSING IN ON HIM.

"RIGHTY" THE RHINO REMEMBERED WHEN ALL WAS PEACEFUL AND RIGHT IN HIS ENVIRONMENT. FEW OF HIS FELLOW RHINOS WERE LEFT. MANY HAD BEEN KILLED MERELY FOR THEIR HORNS AND THEN LEFT FOR DEAD. OTHERS BECAME FEARFUL AND FLED RIGHT AWAY.

ENDANGERED (MEANING VERY FEW OF THEIR SPECIES ARE LEFT) LIONS LIKE "LEFTY" AND RHINOS LIKE "RIGHTY" COULD HAVE LEFT US FOREVER. BUT HUMANS ARE DOING THE RIGHTEOUS THING AND HAVE RECENTLY LEFT THEM ALONE. TODAY THERE ARE LAWS PROTECTING ANIMALS' RIGHTS TO BE LEFT FREE TO INTERACT HARMONIOUSLY WITH NATURE'S CYCLES.

YOU CAN HELP "LEFTY" AND "RIGHTY" AND MANY OTHER THREATENED AND ENDANGERED SPECIES. WE ALL HAVE A RIGHT TO BE CONCERNED THAT THERE MIGHT NOT HAVE BEEN ANY LIONS OR RHINOS LEFT TO GRACE OUR WORLD. ONCE YOU HAVE LEFT SCHOOL TODAY, SIMPLY WRITE TO AGENCIES LISTED IN THE BACK OF THIS BOOK. ALL RIGHT!

Window Terrarium Greenhouse

Question

Can you create your own miniature greenhouse that will allow you to observe the growth of your own plant that you started as a seedling?

Setting the Stage

- Tell students that the greenhouse effect is caused by the sun's rays becoming trapped in our atmosphere, thus increasing the temperature of the air. This could lead to global warming, which can lead to all sorts of imbalances on earth: for example, glacial melting, sea levels rising, and global climatic changes.
- Students can demonstrate and experience the greenhouse effect themselves by planting seedlings in plastic baggies.

Materials Needed for Each Individual

- closable plastic baggie
- thermometer
- soil

- seedlings
- water (see procedure 2)
- colored markers or crayons

- scissors
- window terrarium pattern (page 63)

Procedure

1. Have students add a small amount of soil in the bottom of a baggie. Then they can add their seedling or plant start.
2. Adding one drop of bleach to the soil will prevent mold growth. You can add this to the water bottles that students will use to moisten their soil.
3. Students should cut out their window terrarium pattern and place the baggie in the big window opening (center of pattern).
4. You may choose to have them use a cut-out rule, as shown below, so they can measure the growth of their plant's roots and stems over the next couple of weeks.

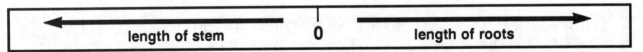

| ← **length of stem** | **0** | **length of roots** → |

5. Tell students that this ruler should be placed vertically along the pattern edge so that it is lined up with the baggie. Zero represents the location of the seed. Increments to be measured should be in inches (centimeters).
6. Teachers may wish to place a thermometer in one of the baggies, a thermometer inside the classroom, and a thermometer outside the classroom. This way the class can make observations of temperature. The temperature in the baggie will be greater due to the greenhouse effect.

Extensions

Have students record plant growth (roots and stems) over the next two weeks. Change variables so that your class can make comparisons, record data, and formulate conclusions.

Closure

In their endangered species journals, have students provide drawings and explanations of the greenhouse effect.

Window Terrarium Greenhouse *(cont.)*

Cut out terrarium pattern.

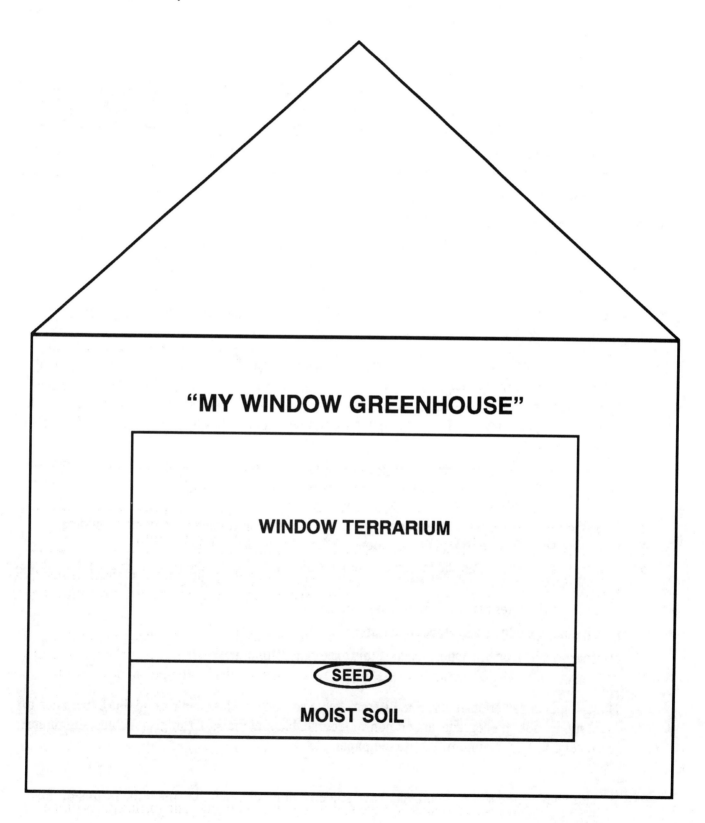

"MY WINDOW GREENHOUSE"

WINDOW TERRARIUM

SEED

MOIST SOIL

Products: Short-lived or Long-lived

Question

Can you find out which trash products are safest for our environment because they are *biodegradable*, meaning that they will be recycled by the earth?

Setting the Stage

- Tell students some types of trash are naturally recycled by nature, such as leaves, orange and banana peels, and most paper products. These materials are considered biodegradable because nature can naturally break them down and recycle them. Products that must be burned or tend to pile up in landfills because they are not biodegradable include styrofoam and many plastics.

- Have the class discuss products that generate trash. From the discussion, list the common trash items students think of. Have the students predict which of these items they believe will naturally break down and which will not.

Materials Needed for Each Group

- large aquarium 20-50 gal (80-200 L)
- dirt or potting soil
- water and a watering container
- plastic
- styrofoam
- paper
- cardboard
- data-capture sheet (page 65), one per student

Procedure

1. Have students place a piece of plastic, styrofoam, cardboard, leaf, and paper on top of dirt that is part way filling an aquarium.

2. Have students bury these materials with dirt. Since we do not know what will happen to the materials or what they will look like weeks from now, explain the importance of identifying them by labeling each A,B,C, etc.

3. Discuss with students that whether or not nature can recycle these materials, things like this take time. Ask students if they can think of anything that could speed up the process—for example, microorganisms, decomposers, weather, moisture, heat, etc.

4. Over the next few weeks have students water the dirt to keep it moist. Students should be recording what they are doing or have done so far on their data-capture sheets.

5. After a few weeks, dig up the materials and have students observe the results. Have them answer these questions:

   - How did these results compare to what you predicted?
   - What happened to each of the materials?
   - What will happen to each material if this experience continues?

Extension

Have students gather other trash items from home so that the class can extend this experience to learn more about biodegradable and non-biodegradable materials. Examples include aluminum cans, cellophane, aluminum foil, waxed paper, etc.

Closure

In their endangered species journals, have students draw pictures to explain the results of their experience.

Products: Short-lived or Long-lived *(cont.)*

Fill in the chart and answer the following questions.

	ITEM A PLASTIC		ITEM B STYROFOAM		ITEM C CARDBOARD		ITEM D LEAF		ITEM E PAPER	
WEEK 1										
• What do you predict?										
• What happens?										
WEEK 2										
• What do you predict?										
• What happens?										
WEEK 3										
• What do you predict?										
• What happens?										
WEEK 4										
• What do you predict?										
• What happens?										

Classroom Recycling Bins

Questions

- Can your class create some practical bins for storing safe trash materials to be recycled effectively and efficiently?
- Can collecting recyclable materials help preserve our environment and do some of these materials contribute to the endangerment of species?

Setting the Stage

Discuss with students how we consumers produce trash each day. Tell students that many materials that we produce are contained, served, or marketed in plastic, paper, aluminum, and styrofoam.

Materials Needed for Each Group

- large box
- heavy duty string or fishing line
- colored markers or crayons
- glue stick
- construction paper
- data-capture sheet (page 67), one per student

Procedure

1. Have each student group take the time to decorate and label their recycling bins. They should depict a thematic representation of recycling and the preservation of our environment.
2. Students can mark right on the boxes or use construction paper and crayons or markers and then mount them on the boxes for decoration using a glue stick.
3. The teacher should poke four small holes in each group's box. The holes will be located at the top center of each face of the box showing (front, back and the two sides).
4. Students can place the string or fishing line (two pieces) through each of the opposite holes. Garbage bags will be placed on top of the line if the group is collecting containers, and nothing is needed on top of the line if newspaper or paper is being collected.
5. Tell students the string or line will prove very helpful when trying to remove the contents of each recycling bin once they are full. Of course, we will want to use the bins over and over again.
6. When the paper or garbage bag is placed on top of the string or line, students can pull the line from the holes and gently lift the contents of their recycling bin. Then the recycling bin is ready to be used once again.
7. While students are involved in this experience, have them work on their data-capture sheets in class and at home.

Extensions

- Students can produce banners, petitions, murals, and/or posters representing similar issues.
- Your class can campaign on the subject of environmental protection and species preservation.

Closure

Have students write to agencies and organizations telling them of their efforts and the results of their campaign. Then have them place copies of their letters in their endangered species journals.

Classroom Recycling Bins *(cont.)*

Fill in the chart with the needed information.

My Home and School Environmental Awareness Check Lists

AT HOME:	USUALLY	SOMETIMES	SELDOM
I TURN OFF LIGHTS WHEN I AM NOT USING THEM.			
I CONSERVE BATH WATER AND DON'T OVERWATER YARD.			
I RECYCLE PAPER, CANS, AND BOTTLES.			
I REUSE PLASTIC, FOIL AND PAPER BAGS.			

AT SCHOOL:	USUALLY	SOMETIMES	SELDOM
I DO NOT LITTER THE HALLS OR PLAYGROUND.			
I USE BOTH SIDES OF WRITING AND DRAWING PAPER.			
I CARPOOL WITH OTHER FAMILIES AND FRIENDS.			
I DO MY BEST TO CONSERVE ENERGY & PRESERVE NATURE.			

Observe

Before you begin your investigation, write your group members' names by their jobs below.

_____Team Leader　　_____Stenographer

_____Biologist　　　　_____Transcriber

Read student information heading, "Natural Selection," below and determine ways that many organisms through time have changed physically (color, body design, beak shape, etc.).

In areas close to your station, time each other for 30 seconds or one minute as each of you tries to locate as many butterfly patterns as you can. Answer these questions on the back of this paper. Watch closely, for some may be easier to find than others. Why? How does color of an organism help prevent its destruction? Explain. What is meant by *camouflage*?

NATURAL SELECTION

The process of natural selection refers to apparent changes species have undergone through time in order to survive in a dynamic system. For instance, it has been observed that beaks of certain birds have changed in shape and function to suit a changing environment. Also, amphibians are believed to have developed lungs as adults so they could inhabit land in a time when water environments were overpopulated and food was scarce.

"Survival of the fittest" is a scientific theory suggesting that, through time, those species that have survived have adapted to an ever-changing world and those that have become extinct were unable to accommodate change quickly or adequately enough. It is interesting to note that some species such as sharks appear to have changed little over millions of years.

Put your finished activity paper in the collection pocket on the side of the table at this station.

Note to the teacher: Use the butterfly pattern sheet to copy several butterflies of different species and color them in. Place strategically around the station or center area. Be sure to include some that are strong contrasts to the background and other shades that blend in nicely with the background.

Observe *(cont.)*

Copy, color, and cut out butterfly patterns.

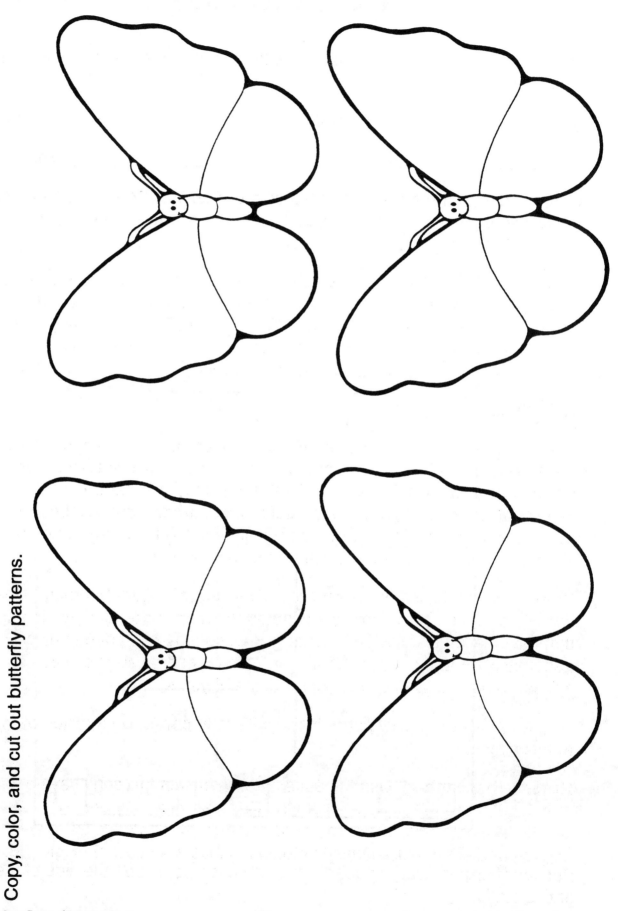

Communicate

Before beginning your investigation, write your group members' names by their jobs below.

_____Team Leader   _____Stenographer

_____Biologist   _____Transcriber

Can you decipher the coded puzzles below? Each puzzle spells out a word describing the eating habits of animals in the wild. Good luck!

B	E	R
R	I	O
H	E	V

R	V	I
A	O	C
N	E	R

Put your finished activity paper in the collection pocket on the side of the table at this station.

Compare

Before beginning your investigation, write your group members' names by their jobs below.

_____Team Leader   _____Stenographer

_____Biologist   _____Transcriber

Many animals have very acute senses, such as smelling, hearing, and seeing. They have developed these senses over time as a means of surviving. For instance, many animals are warned of predators quickly enough to flee because they hear, see, or smell them. Also, many predator animals would starve if not for their keen senses to help them locate food.

To compare your sense of sight to that of a predator animal, follow the steps below:

1. Test and measure the distance of your limited sight by placing a colored, wooden block 1" x 1" (2.5 cm x 2.5 cm) on the ground.

2. Back away slowly from the block and measure, in yards (meters), the distance you are away from the block when you can no longer see it.

3. Multiply this value by eight. This will give you the distance at which predator birds such as eagles can detect their prey.

4. How far were you able to back up before you could no longer see the wooden block?_____

5. How far away can an eagle see the block?_____

   Now you see why an eagle is such a great hunter!

   Put your finished activity paper in the collection pocket on the side of the table at this station.

Order

Before beginning your investigation, write your group members' names by their jobs below.

_____Team Leader   _____Stenographer

_____Biologist   _____Transcriber

In the food pyramid below, organize each level according to its particular function or role. Begin by arranging, in order, the list of species provided. Complete by drawing and labeling each species in its appropriate placement or level on the food pyramid.

> hawk, mosquito larvae, plankton, minnows, algae, turtle, bass, worm,
> green plant leaves, spider, aphid, duck, mouse, lettuce, humans

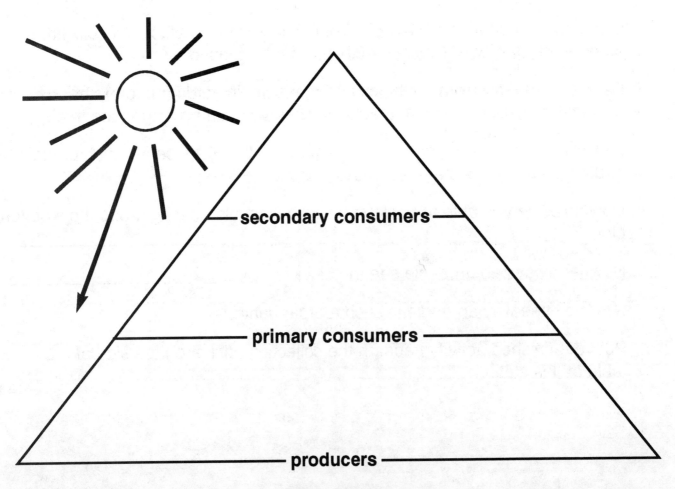

Put your finished activity paper in the collection pocket on the side of the table at this station.

Categorize

Before beginning your investigation, write your group members' names by their jobs below.

_____Team Leader   _____Stenographer

_____Biologist   _____Transcriber

There are living and nonliving things in this world. Living things are plants, animals, insects, and bacteria. These living organisms are all made up of cells. They require food, water, and air to survive. Most living things are able to move or get around. Some accomplish this with limbs, fins, or wings. Most living organisms also must obtain food. Some catch their food, some make their own food using light energy from the sun, and some get their food by absorbing nutrients from the earth or decaying things.

Nonliving things are things that do not need food, water, or air to survive. These things are made from atoms. They are solids, liquids, or gases. Examples include rocks, soil, plastic, glass, cement, and metals.

As you take a tour of your schoolyard or your own backyard, look for examples of living and nonliving things. List them below and describe why you think they are one or the other.

LIVING

NONLIVING

Put your finished activity paper in the collection pocket on the side of the table at this station.

Relate

Before beginning your investigation, write your group members' names by their jobs below.

_____Team Leader   _____Stenographer

_____Biologist   _____Transcriber

Match the picture of the living organisms below with the statement telling why they are endangered.

Some people like to wear boots or belts made from my skin.

People keep clearing us and decreasing our numbers in order to make room for more and more people.

During history, humans have overhunted us at an alarming rate. For a while, we were almost gone forever.

Humans have feared us throughout history and have conquered us to prove their superiority.

Many people like us for our soft, warm fur, even though there are many products for sale that can do the same job.

Put your finished activity paper in the collection pocket on the side of the table at this station.

Infer

Before beginning your investigation, write your group members' names by their jobs below.

_____Team Leader   _____Stenographer

_____Biologist   _____Transcriber

In the year 1800 the world's population was one billion people.
In the year 1900 the world's population was two billion people.
In the year 2000 the world's population will be six billion people.

Graph this information on the chart below.

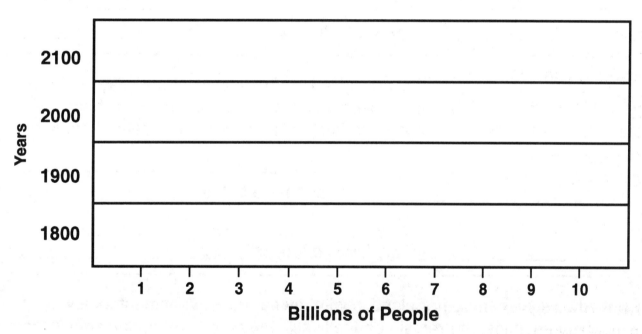

1. Based on your graph, what do you predict the world population will be in another 100 years?_____

2. Why?_____

3. Use a new color to graph your prediction above.

Put your finished activity paper in the collection pocket on the side of the table at this station.

Apply

Before beginning your investigation, write your group members' names by their jobs below.

_____Team Leader   _____Stenographer

_____Biologist   _____Transcriber

When I am escaping from a predator, I squirt dark ink at my enemy. For a moment this confuses them and they lose track of me. For the short time that they cannot see me, I slip away safely. Who am I?

I am a_____, and I live in the_____.
I have many predators, such as_____and
_____. My favorite food is_____.

I hang out in large groups of my own kind. You know what they say—"There is power in numbers." If one of us becomes alerted to danger, we all become alerted. Our numbers will always be fairly high, because our natural predators can't get us all.

I am a_____, and I live in the_____.
I have many predators, such as_____and
_____. My favorite food is_____.

I cleverly disguise myself or blend in with my natural environment as a way of fooling my enemies. If I remain perfectly still, they might go right by me without being aware of my presence. Soon they will give up, and I can be on my way.

I am a_____, and I live in the_____.
I have many predators, such as_____and
_____. My favorite food is_____.

Put your finished activity paper in the collection pocket on the side of the table at this station.

Apply *(cont.)*

To scare my predators I make them think that I am bigger and scarier than I really am. I have markings on my wings that are big and round. When I open my wings my enemies think they are seeing a big head with large eyes.

I am a_____, and I live in the_____.
I have many predators, such as_____and
_____. My favorite food is_____.

As a class, make up the next two together or work in groups and try to stump your friends or other classmates. Be sure to describe a creative and/or unique adaptation or behavior of a plant or animal that makes it special. Have fun!

I am a_____, and I live in the_____.
I have many predators, such as_____and
_____. My favorite food is _____.

I am a_____, and I live in the_____.
I have many predators, such as_____and
_____. My favorite food is _____.

Put your finished activity paper in the collection pocket on the side of the table at this station.

Science Safety

Discuss the necessity for science safety rules. Reinforce the rules on this page or adapt them to meet the needs of your classroom. You may wish to reproduce the rules for each student or post them in the classroom.

1. Begin science activities only after all directions have been given.

2. Never put anything in your mouth unless it is required by the science experience.

3. Always wear safety goggles when participating in any lab experience.

4. Dispose of waste and recyclables in proper containers.

5. Follow classroom rules of behavior while participating In science experiences.

6. Review your basic class safety rules every time you conduct a science experience.

You can still have fun and be safe at the same time!

Endangered Species Journal

Endangered Species Journals are an effective way to integrate science and language arts. Students are to record their observations, thoughts, and questions about past science experiences in a journal to be kept in the science area. The observations may be recorded in sentences or sketches which keep track of changes both in the science item or in the thoughts and discussions of the students.

Endangered Species Journal entries can be completed as a team effort or an individual activity. Be sure to model the making and recording of observations several times when introducing the journals to the science area.

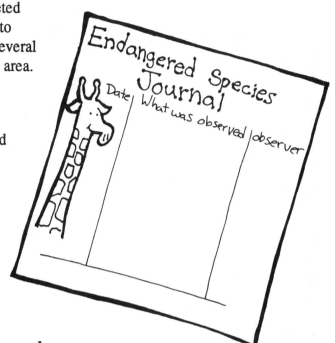

Use the student recordings in the Endangered Species Journals as a focus for class science discussions. You should lead these discussions and guide students with probing questions, but it is usually not necessary for you to give any explanation. Students come to accurate conclusions as a result of classmates' comments and your questioning. Endangered Species Journals can also become part of the students' portfolios and overall assessment program. Journals are valuable assessment tools for parent and student conferences as well.

How To Make an Endangered Species Journal

1. Cut two pieces of 8.5" x 11" (22 cm x 28 cm) construction paper to create a cover. Reproduce page 80 and glue it to the front cover of the journal. Allow students to draw endangered species pictures in the box on the cover.
2. Insert several Endangered Species Journal pages. (See page 81.)
3. Staple together and cover stapled edge with book tape.

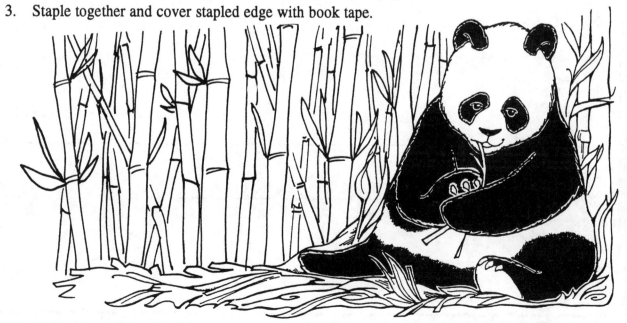

My
Endangered Species
Journal

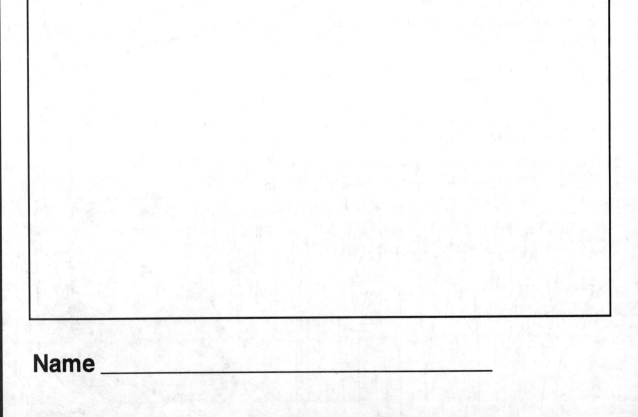

Name _____

Endangered Species Journal

Illustration

This is what happened: _____

_____

_____

_____

_____

This is what I learned: _____

_____

_____

_____

My Science Activity

K-W-L Strategy

Answer each question about the topic you have chosen.

Topic: _____

K- What I already **know:** _____

_____

_____

_____

_____

W- What I **want to find out:** _____

_____

_____

_____

_____

L- What I **learned after doing the activity:** _____

_____

_____

_____

_____

Investigation Planner *(Option 1)*

Observation

_____

_____

Question

_____

_____

Hypothesis

_____

_____

Procedure

Materials Needed:

_____

_____

_____

_____

Step-by-Step Directions:(Number each step!)

_____

_____

_____

_____

_____

Investigation Planner *(Option 2)*

Science Experience Form

Scientist _____

Title of Activity _____

Observation: What caused us to ask the question?

_____

_____

_____

Question: What do we want to find out?

_____

_____

_____

Hypothesis: What do we think we will find out?

_____

_____

_____

Procedure: How will we find out? (List step-by-step.)

_____

_____

_____

_____

Results: What actually happened?

_____

_____

_____

Conclusions: What did we learn?

_____

_____

Endangered Species Observation Area

In addition to station-to-station activities, students should be given other opportunities for real-life science experiences. For example, a mini computer and terrarium can provide a vehicle for discovery learning if students are given enough time and space to observe them.

Set up an endangered species observation area in your classroom. As children visit this area during open work time, expect to hear stimulating conversations and questions among them. Encourage curiosity but respect their independence!

Books with facts pertinent to the subject, item, or process being observed should be provided for students who are ready to research more sophisticated information.

Sometimes it is very stimulating to set up a science experiment or add something interesting to the Endangered Species observation area without a comment from you at all! If the experiment or materials in the observation area should not be disturbed, reinforce with students the need to observe without touching or picking up.

Assessment Forms

The following chart can be used by the teacher to rate cooperative-learning groups in a variety of settings.

Science Groups Evaluation Sheet

Room: _____   Date: _____

Activity: _____

Everyone

. . . gets started.

. . . participates.

. . . knows jobs.

. . . solves group problems.

. . . cooperates.

. . . keeps noise down.

. . . encourages others.

Group									
1	2	3	4	5	6	7	8	9	10

Teacher comment

_____

Bragging rights for the group session: _____

_____

Assessment Forms *(cont.)*

The evaluation form below provides student groups with the opportunity to evaluate the group's overall success.

Cooperative Group Evaluation

Assignment: _____

Date: _____

Scientists	Jobs
_____	_____
_____	_____
_____	_____
_____	_____

As a group, decide which face you should fill in and complete the remaining sentences.

1. We finished our assignment on time, and we did a good job.

2. We encouraged each other, and we cooperated with each other.

3. We did best at _____

_____ .

4. Next time we could improve at _____

_____ .

Assessment Forms *(cont.)*

The following form may be used as part of the assessment process for hands-on science experiences.

Science Anecdotal Record Form

Date: _____

Scientist's Name: _____

Topic: _____

Assessment Situation: _____

Instructional Task: _____

Behavior/Skill Observed: _____

_____

_____

_____

_____

_____

This behavior/skill is important because _____

_____

_____

_____

_____ .

Super Biologist Award

This is to certify that

_____

Name

made a science discovery.

Congratulations!

_____

Teacher

_____

Date

Organizations and Agencies

There are several worthwhile efforts by organizations and agencies to protect endangered wildlife. To find out how you can get involved and help with their efforts, write to them. Their addresses are below. Be sure to include your name, school, and why you are writing to them.

Animal Welfare Institute P.O. Box 3650 Washington, DC 20007	Earth Island Institute 300 Broadway, Ste. 28 San Francisco, CA 94133-3313
Center for Marine Conservation 1725 DeSales Street, NW, #500 Washington, DC 20036	Environmental Defense Fund 257 Park Ave. South New York, NY 10010
Defenders of Wildlife 1244 19th Street, NW Washington, DC 20036	Greenpeace USA 1436 U Street, NW Washington, DC 20009

Organizations and Agencies *(cont.)*

National Arbor Day Foundation
100 Arbor Ave.
Nebraska City, NE 68410

National Wildlife Federation
8925 Leesburg Pike
Vienna, VA 22184-0001

National Geographic Society
17th and M Streets, NW
Washington, DC 20036

The Sierra Club
Public Affairs Department
730 Polk Street
San Francisco, CA 94109

National Parks Service
Department of the Interior
Office of Public Affairs
P.O. Box 37127
Washington, DC 20013-7127

U.S. Environmental Protection
Agency
401 M Street, SW
Washington, DC 20460

Natural Resources Defense Council
90 New Montgomery Street, Ste. 620
San Francisco, CA 94105

Wilderness Society
900 17th Street, NW
Washington, DC 20006-2596

Threatened, Endangered, and Extinct Species

Threatened

Plants or animals most likely to become endangered due to their numbers, loss of habitat, food supply, or human-induced circumstances. They include:

- Aleutian Canada goose
- alligator
- eastern indigo snake
- leopard darter
- desert tortoise
- valley elderberry
- longhorn beetle
- grizzly bear
- northeastern beach tiger beetle
- puritan tiger beetle
- Queen Alexandra birdwing (largest butterfly)
- noonday snail
- loggerhead sea turtle
- greater sandhill crane
- Shasta salamander
- rough sculpin (small fish)
- Trinity bristle snail
- bighorn sheep
- wolverine
- Sierra Nevada red fox
- Little Kern golden trout
- Lalontan cutthroat trout
- Painte cutthroat trout
- San Joaquin antelope squirrel
- Swanson's hawk
- Guadalupe fur seal
- Steller sea lion
- southern sea otter
- southern rubber boa
- black toad
- Cottonball Marsh pupfish

Endangered

Those plants and animals in danger of becoming extinct, gone forever, due to their critically low numbers, loss of habitat, dwindling food supply, and human-induced circumstances. They include:

- badger
- brown pelican
- bullfrog
- California condor
- cheetah
- crocodile
- dolphins
- eagle (bald and golden)
- elephants (African and Indian)
- falcon (peregrine)
- giant kangaroo rat
- gila monster
- giraffe
- ivory billed woodpecker
- kangaroo
- kit fox
- loon
- manatee
- mountain lion
- northern spotted owl
- orangutan
- orchid
- panda
- pitcher plant
- polar bear
- sea turtle
- seal (harp and monk)
- snow leopard
- tigers (bengal and siberian)
- timber wolf
- trumpeter swan
- whales (7 different species)
- whooping crane
- wild mustang
- zebra

Extinct

Those plants and animals which are extinct, gone forever.
They include:

- Alossa fritillory butterfly
- Antioch rubber fly
- Antioch shield-back katydid
- Antioch Spesid wasp
- Clear Lake splittail
- dinosaurs
- do-do bird
- El Segundo flower-loving fly
- long eared kit fox
- Mono Lake hygratus diving beetle
- oblivious tiger beetle
- Pasadena freshwater shrimp
- passenger pigeon
- saber toothed tiger
- San Clemente's Bewick's wren
- San Joaquin Valley tiger beetle
- Santa Barbara song sparrow
- sooty crawfish
- Sthenele satyr butterfly
- Stronbeen's Parnassian butterfly
- Tecopa pupfish
- thick-tail chub
- Valley flower-loving fly
- wooly mammoth
- Xerces blue butterfly
- yellow-banded Andrid bee

Glossary

Acid Rain—the results of combining sulfur dioxide and nitrogen oxide with water droplets in the atmosphere.

Adaptation—any feature or trait an organism acquires which increases its chances of survival in its surroundings.

Biome—a large region of earth characterized by certain climatic conditions and specific plant and animal populations.

Biosphere—the part of the earth's crust, water, and atmosphere where living organisms can exist and flourish.

Camouflage—the ability of an organism to blend into its environment for protection.

Carnivore—an animal that relies on meat to survive. Carnivores are considered secondary consumers.

Conclusion—the outcome of an investigation.

Conservation—the wise and intelligent use or protection of natural resources and wildlife.

Consumer—in a food chain the consumer utilizes the producer for its food. Consumers depend on the consumption of plants and/or animals for survival.

Control—a standard measure of comparison in an experiment. The control always stays the same.

Diversity—the biological difference among living organisms and their environments.

Ecologist—a scientist who studies the relationships among organisms and their environments.

Ecosystem—a system by which all the living things comprising it depend on one another for survival.

Endangered—plants and animals which are not replenishing their species as quickly as they are dying off.

Environment—the total of all of the surroundings—air, water, vegetation, and wildlife—that has influence on one's existence.

Erosion—the carrying away of earth's warm materials by water, ice, and/or wind.

Experiment—a means of proving or disproving an hypothesis.

Extinct—the condition of those plant and/or animal species that no longer exist.

Food Chain—the natural predator-prey course of survival for organisms of a given ecosystem.

Food Web—an interlocking pattern of food chains often consisting of plants or animals representative of more than one food chain within the web.

Global Warming—the heating up of the earth's atmosphere beyond normal levels.

Greenhouse Effect—a term used to describe how the gases in the earth's atmosphere trap the sun's warmth.

Grouping—the tendency of many life forms, resulting from adaptation, to group together in large numbers.

Habitat—the most suitable natural environment or living space for a particular plant or animal species.

Glossary *(cont.)*

H
I
M
N
O

P

Q
R
S

T
V
W

Herbivore—any living creature dependent upon plants for survival. Herbivores are considered primary consumers.

Hypothesis (hi-POTH-e-sis)—an educated guess to a question you are trying to answer.

Investigation—observation of something followed by a systematic inquiry in order to explain what was originally observed.

Migration—to move regularly to a different place at a certain time of year.

Niche—the environment or habitat to which a particular species belongs or has adapted to.

Observation—careful notice or examination of something.

Omnivore—living things that consume both plants and animals for survival.

Ozone Layer—the natural protective layer of the atmosphere which blocks out and absorbs the energy of ultra-violet radiation emitted by the sun. Ozone is chemically represented as O_3.

Pesticide—any chemical preparation, such as DDT, used to control populations of organisms perceived to be harmful or a nuisance.

Photosynthesis—the process by which plants absorb light energy and convert the energy into needed food.

Pollution—harmful substances deposited in the air, water, and land leading to a state of unhealthiness and uncleanliness.

Predator—an animal that kills other animals for survival.

Prey—refers to those animals lower on the food chain.

Procedure—the series of steps carried out when doing an experiment.

Producers—on a food pyramid, or in a food chain, the organisms responsible for producing their own food from the sun's energy.

Question—a formal way of inquiring about a particular topic.

Recycle—the reuse of paper, plastic, metal, and other substances commonly utilized by people.

Results—the data collected after performing an experiment.

Scientific Method—a creative and systematic process of proving or disproving a given question, following an observation. Observation, question, hypothesis, procedure, results, conclusion, and future investigations.

Scientific-Process Skills—the skills necessary to have in order to be able to think critically. Process skills include: observing, communicating, comparing, ordering, categorizing, relating, inferring, and applying.

Threatened—plants and animals that one can easily predict are going to become endangered unless current circumstances change.

Variable—the changing factor of an experiment.

Weathering—the breaking down or washing away of the earth's rocks, minerals, and deposits by water, ice, and wind.

Bibliography

Althea. *Rainforest Homes.* Cambridge U Pr., 1985.

Arnold, Caroline. *A Walk in the Desert.* Silver Press, 1990.

        A Walk up the Mountain. Silver Press, 1990.

        A Walk by the Seashore. Silver Press, 1990.

        A Walk in the Woods. Silver Press, 1990.

Bare, Colleen Stanley. *Never Kiss an Alligator.* Dutton, 1989.

Baylor, Byrd. *Hawk, I'm Your Brother.* Charles Scribner Sons, 1976.

Berger, Melvin. *Animals in Hiding.* Newbridge Comms, 1993.

Cherry, Lynne. *The Great Kapok Tree: Tale of the Amazon Rainforest.* Harcourt, Brace, and Jovanovich, 1990.

Chinery, Michael. *Rainforest Animals.* Random Bks Yng Read., 1992.

Cook, Shirley. *Endangered Species Linking: Environmental Studies with Everyday Life.* Incentive Publications, 1993.

Costa de Beauregard, Diane. *Animals in Jeopardy.* Young Discovery Lib., 1991.

Cuthbert, Susan. *Endangered Creatures.* Lion USA, 1992.

Dixon, Dougal. *When Dinosaurs Ruled the Earth.* Gareth Stevens, 1989.

Ernst, Kathryn. *Mr. Tamarin's Trees.* Crown Publishers, 1976.

George, Jean Craighead. *The Talking Earth.* Harper Collins, 1983.

Helen, Ruth. *How to Hide a Polar Bear and Other Mammals.* Putman, 1986.

Hirshie, Ron. *Who Lives in the Forest.* Putnam, 1986.

Landau, Elaine. *Endangered Plants.* Watts, 1992.

Love, Ann and Jane Drake. *Take Action: An Environmental Book for Kids.* World Wildlife Federation, 1992.

Margolies, Barbara. *Rehema's Journey: A Visit to Tanzania.* Scholastic, 1990.

Morris, Dean. *Endangered Animals.* Raintree Steck-V, 1990.

National Wildlife Federation Staff. *Endangered Species.* Natl. Wildlife, 1991.

Powzyk, Joyce. *Tracking Wild Chimpanzees.* Lothrop, Lee & Shepard, 1990.

Provensen, Alice. *The Year at Maple Hill Farm.* McMillian, 1988.

Roy, Ronald. *A Thousand Pails of Water.* Knopf, 1978.

Stone, Lynn. *Endangered Animals.* Childrens, 1984.

Suess. *The Lorax.* Lectorum, 1992.

Taylor, Dave. *Endangered Desert Animals.* Crabtree Pub. Co., 1992.

        Endangered Forest Animals. Crabtree Pub. Co., 1992.

        Endangered Grassland Animals. Crabtree Pub. Co., 1992.

        Endangered Island Animals. Crabtree Pub. Co., 1992.

        Endangered Mountain Animals. Crabtree Pub. Co., 1992.

        Endangered Ocean Animals. Crabtree Pub. Co., 1992.

Bibliography *(cont.)*

Taylor, Mildred. *Song of Trees.* Dial Press, 1975.

Turner, Ann. *Heron Street.* Harper, 1989.

Uchitel, Sandra & Serge Michaels. *Endangered Animals of the Rain Forests.* Price Stern, 1992.

Yoshida, Toshi. *Young Lions.* Philomel, 1989.

Endangered Animals. Educ Insights, 1992.

Endangered Birds: An Educational Coloring Book. Spizzirri, 1992.

Endangered Young'uns. Antioch Pub Co., 1991.

Endangered Wildlife of the World. Marshall Cavendish, 1993.

Kid Heroes of the Environment: Simple Things Real Kids are Doing to Save the Earth. Earth Works Press, 1992.

Spanish Titles

Bornemann, E. *¡Nada de tucanes! (No Toucans Allowed!).* Lectorum, 1987.

Cole, J. *El autobus magico viaja por el agua (Magic School Bus Inside the Waterworks).* Scholastic, 1986.

Cowcher, H. *La tigresa (Tigress).* Farrar, Strauss, & Giroux, 1993.

Suess. *El Lorax (The Lorax).* Lectorum, 1993.

Wright, A. *¿Les echaremos de menos? Especies en peligro de extincion (Will We Miss Them? Species in Danger of Extinction).* Charlesbridge Publishing, 1992.

Technology

Cornet. *Animals of the World Series: Animals of a Living Reef, Animals of North America, and Animals of South America.* Available from Cornet/MTI Film & Video, (800)777-8100. video

Inview. *A Field Trip to the Rainforest.* Available from Sunburst, (800)321-7511. software

Learningways, Inc. *Whales and Wolves.* Available from William K. Bradford Publishing Co., (800)421-2009. software

National Geographic Series. *STV: Rain Forest.* Available from VideoDiscovery, (800)548-3472. videodisc

Orange Cherry. *Talking Jungle Safari.* Available from CDL Software Shop, (800)637-0047. software

Partridge Film & Video. *Monkey Rain Forest.* Available from Cornet/MTI Film & Video, (800)777-8100. videodisc

Troll. *I Can Read About Animals: Whales and Dolphins.* Available from CDL Software Shop, (800)637-0047. software